WITHDRAWN

TRAGEDY IN FRANCE

Other Books by André Maurois

ARIEL

BYRON

CAPTAINS AND KINGS

DISRAELI

MAPE

LYAUTEY

THE SILENCE OF COLONEL BRAMBLE

GENERAL BRAMBLE

DICKENS

PROPHETS AND POETS

THE THOUGHT READING MACHINE

RICOCHETS

THE MIRACLE OF ENGLAND

CHATEAUBRIAND

THE ART OF LIVING

TRAGEDY
IN FRANCE

By

André Maurois

Translated from the French by

DENVER LINDLEY

HARPER & BROTHERS *Publishers*
New York *and* London

94844

CONTENTS

I

Foreword   vii

I. *Why France and England Were Ill-Prepared for War*   3

II. *Why the First Eight Months of the War Were Wasted*   27

III. *How the Clash of Personalities Impeded the Conduct of the War*   62

IV. *Why the German Offensive Was So Quickly Successful*   90

V. *How France and England Were Separated*   125

VI. *What Happened to France*   158

II

NOTES AND OBSERVATIONS

Ten Commandments for British Soldiers in France   189
Ten Commandments for the Civilian in Time of War   193
King George Visits His Armies   197

[v]

CONTENTS

Reconnaissance Squadron   205
A Stroll with the Padre   211
The British Army in Training   217
First Days in Belgium   233
Royal Air Force   243
The Spirit of France   249

FOREWORD

I ARRIVED in America on July 18, 1940. I had spent
the duration of the war with the British and French
armies and then, on June 10th, had been sent on a
mission to London. I had, alas, observed France
and England during tragic moments; I had known
many of the men who governed the two countries
and many of those who commanded their armies.
Naturally, I was besieged with questions by my
American friends. After the very first of these con-
versations it was clear to me that, on many subjects,
unfounded rumors had gained credence even in the
minds of those whose good faith was beyond question. I believed the truth, distressing though it
might appear to me, was infinitely less dangerous
for my country than accounts distorted by passion.
I have not by any means seen and known everything

[vii]

FOREWORD

and I neither can write, nor wish to write, the history of this war, but I can and should give my testimony. I have done my best to make it objective and impartial.

ANDRÉ MAUROIS

I

TRANSLATED BY DENVER LINDLEY

I

WHY FRANCE AND ENGLAND WERE ILL-PREPARED FOR WAR

ONE DAY toward the end of 1935 I had lunch in London at the home of Lady Leslie in company with Winston Churchill, my hostess' nephew. After the meal he took me by the arm and led me into a small room.

"Now, Mr. Maurois," he said brusquely, "you must not write any more novels. No! And you must not write any more biographies. No!"

I looked at him in some alarm.

"All you must do now," he went on, "is to write one article a day, a single article, and the same one every day. Articles in which you will express, in all the different ways you can think of, a single idea: the French air force, which used to be the best in

[3]

the world, is slipping back to fourth or fifth place. The German air force, which used to be non-existent, is in process of becoming the best in the world. Nothing else. And if you proclaim these truths in France, and if you force France to listen to them, you will have performed a much greater service than in describing a woman's loves or a man's ambitions."

I replied that, unfortunately, I was by no means an expert in aviation, that I had no authority to talk about it, that no one would listen to me if I did, and that, consequently, despite his advice, I should continue to write novels and biographies.

"You will be wrong," he said in his vigorous and ironic voice, to which from time to time a slight difficulty in enunciation gave a pleasant and characteristic flavor. "You will be wrong. At this moment the threat embodied in the German air force is the *one* theme that should interest a Frenchman. For your country may die because of it. Culture and literature, Mr. Maurois, are all very well, but a culture without strength soon ceases to be a living culture."

I never wrote the articles Winston Churchill ad-

vised me to write and today I bitterly regret it. But
that conversation impressed me greatly and left me
with an abiding uneasiness. On several occasions I
made inquiries from qualified persons about the
state of our air force. Each time the reply was either
evasive or frankly pessimistic.

"If the war should break out," I was told by a
colonel in charge of a bombing squadron at Lyon,
"we will die bravely, my pilots and I, but that's all
we can do!"

"Why?" I asked.

"Because there are too few of us and our machines are obsolete."

In 1936 the situation became even worse. Sit-
down strikes in the factories, lack of energy on the
part of the government and the red tape of bureaucracy reduced French production almost to
zero. During the year 1937 the number of airplanes
produced *each month* by French factories fell to
the almost unbelievable figure of *thirty-eight*—at a
time when the monthly production in Germany
was exceeding a *thousand* planes!

While, in France, a deplorable hostility was
poisoning the relations between workmen and the

leaders of industry, in Germany all the forces of the nation had been mobilized for a war of revenge which the German government had foreseen and which it wanted. Absurd stories were circulated in France about the alleged weakness of the Nazi régime. They were examples of wishful thinking. All those who knew Germany well—Sir Eric Phipps, the British Ambassador, for example, and Mr. François-Poncet, the French Ambassador to Berlin—had been reiterating their warnings for years. I remember being present in 1937 during a conversation between these two men.

"Don't have any illusions about it," said François-Poncet. "Germany is strong; she knows it and she is determined to make use of her strength. Two lines of conduct, and only two, are open to France and to Great Britain: either our two countries must renounce everything else and devote all their energies to a formidable rearmament, or they must try to reach an understanding with Germany."

I asked: "But is that possible? Does Germany want an understanding?"

"Germany," François-Poncet replied in the sarcastic voice of a bitter humorist, "Germany wants nothing and wants everything . . . Germany desires to be dynamic, that is, to change. . . . The men who today are her leaders love spectacular celebrations, gigantic symbols. Do you wish to win them over? Build face to face on opposite banks of the Rhine two colossal ladders. On one bank bring up some millions of young Germans carrying flags with the swastika, on the other some millions of young Frenchmen carrying the colors of France; have these young people climb up and down the ladders in faultless formation while, on a float in the middle of the Rhine, General Gamelin meets Hitler. Then perhaps there will be a chance of bringing about an understanding between France and Germany, *if at the same time you have become very strong* . . . But if you carry on your relations with the Reich in terms of diplomatic quibbling and finesse, which it despises, if you continue to draft notes and make speeches instead of building airplanes and tanks, then we are headed straight for war, and for a war that we shall not win."

François-Poncet was not the only one to form an estimate of Germany's new strength. Foreign countries, comparing the Nazis' military expenditures with those of France and England, understood very well that the balance of forces in Europe was going

[7]

to shift—and many of them took precautions. Mr. Laroche, who was French Ambassador to Poland, often said to me that he thought it unjust to blame the Poles for having sought German favor after 1936.

"What could you expect?" he said. "When they saw Germany was rearming and France and England were not making the slightest effort to oppose her, when they saw Hitler, in March, 1936, march his troops into the Rhineland (an action in absolute contravention of the Treaty of Locarno) without France lifting a finger to stop him, when they heard the French Premier say over the radio: 'I shall not allow Strasbourg to remain within range of German guns,' and when they saw with stupefaction that this speech was not followed by any action whatsoever, they lost all confidence in us. The leaders of Poland said to us as early as 1934: 'If you do not prevent Germany from rearming we shall be forced to become her friends.' And at the very time we were losing the confidence of Poland we saw both Belgium and Yugoslavia slip away from us for the same reason."

In this lack of diplomatic preparation and in this

abandonment of Europe to German hegemony the responsibility of Great Britain was at least as great as that of France. Many powerful groups were united in restraining Great Britain from adopting a courageous and foresighted foreign policy. The bankers of the City were concerned about the money they had loaned to Germany and they persisted in the naïve hope that they could do business with a country that was shouting from the roof tops its intention to be self-sufficient. A certain number of persons of importance in England, terrified by Bolshevism, believed foolishly they had found in Nazism a barrier to the Revolution. At the same time the intellectual liberals were preaching peace at any price and unilateral disarmament, which was destined to be the death of liberalism. All these tendencies combined magnificently to play into the hands of Germany.

No doubt the common people in France and England were aware, more or less consciously, of our weakness; for in 1938 they were profoundly hostile to the idea of a war. It was easy to see this at the time of Munich. American public opinion, at that point, was severely critical of Chamberlain and Daladier. But the United States did not know the real situation. They had little idea of the state of mind of the citizens of Paris and London, who saw themselves without air-raid shelters, without gas masks and without antiaircraft guns, while there circulated, thanks to the efficiency of German propaganda, terrifying rumors about two-ton bombs the very breath of which could destroy whole sections of a city, and about poison gases that would be released above them.

Men who would have been bravery itself if they had had to fight in the front line against an enemy like the one of 1914 were terrified at the thought of a war behind the lines in which their wives and children would be the victims. And so the peace of Munich, which New York considered shameful, was received by the crowds in Paris and London with almost unbelievable enthusiasm. This diplomatic abdication was celebrated like a victory. One member of the Paris Municipal Council even dared propose that a street be given the name *Rue de Trente Septembre*, the date of the capitulation.

Mr. Neville Chamberlain had been the principal artisan of the negotiations. It was a strange destiny that brought this Mayor of Birmingham, chairman of numerous boards, a business man accustomed to deal with other business men who considered contracts sacred, face to face with the romantic Chancellor of the Reich, who was convinced he had no duties except to Germany and that an agreement with a foreign nation had no value except in so far as it was useful to the German people. Neville Chamberlain, more insular than any other Englishman, had no idea, before the first interview, that there could be such a man as Adolf Hitler. At the time of his departure for Berchtesgaden one of my English friends said to me:

"Chamberlain doesn't really believe that Adolf Hitler is, like himself, a member of the Birmingham Corporation, but he does believe that he is a member of the Manchester Corporation."

And that was true.

In November, 1938, two months after his meetings with the Fuehrer, Mr. Chamberlain described to some Frenchmen, one evening at the Quai d'Orsay, his reception in Berchtesgaden. Hitler had said to him:

"Shall we talk alone or in front of your associates?"

"Alone," Mr. Chamberlain replied.

Then Hitler took him (with the interpreter, Dr. Schmidt) into his own bedroom. It was a small room furnished with an iron bedstead; on the wall was a single, very fine picture, which came from a museum in Munich and which was changed from time to time. Mr. Chamberlain was stupefied by the torrent of words that constituted the German Chancellor's conversation and by the impossibility of getting in the slightest reply.

"When I arrived in Godesberg for the second interview," Chamberlain said, "I was received with speeches of such violence that almost immediately it seemed clear to me that it would be useless to continue a conversation begun in that tone. Every few minutes (by an obviously prearranged plan) an officer would enter and hand the Fuehrer a dispatch. 'Two more Germans killed by the Czechs,' Hitler would cry, his face contorted with rage. 'All the blood that has been spilled shall be avenged! The Czechs must be annihilated!' Seeing his fury, whether simulated or not, increasing, I said to the interpreter that it would be better to break off the interview and that I would return to my hotel.

Since this was on the opposite bank of the Rhine I had to cross the river by ferry. As I was withdrawing, Hitler, continuing to express himself with the same violence, followed me out onto the terrace. There, suddenly, he stopped speaking, the expression on his face changed with extraordinary rapidity, he looked at the river stretching away at our feet and murmured in a soft, almost tender voice: 'Oh, Mr. Prime Minister, I am so sorry. I had looked forward to showing you this beautiful view . . . but now it is hidden by the mist. . . .' Never have I seen a human being change so abruptly from savage anger to poetic mood."

One of the officials of the Foreign Office who had accompanied Mr. Chamberlain to Germany told me that the Prime Minister had retained a painful impression of these interviews and that such outbursts of violence were something entirely new in his experience so that even now when anyone mentions the name of Hitler in his presence "he makes a face like that of a child who is being forced to swallow castor oil." But Mr. Chamberlain thought it his duty to preserve peace and he hoped he had succeeded.

[13]

He was encouraged in this belief by the innumerable testimonials he received from men and
women in France and England. Thousands of peasant women in our French provinces wrote to thank
him for having saved their country from war, their
homes from bombs and their children from death.
Old women on French farms knitted mittens for
him "so that," they said in their letters, written in
a large, trembling hand, "he would not be cold in
his airplane. . . ." All this appeared infinitely
touching to Mrs. Neville Chamberlain, a sweet and
tender-hearted woman, who encouraged her husband to persevere in the path of appeasement.

That path, after Munich, ceased to be the popular one in England. English public opinion had
been forced to swallow Munich, for want of preparation in the army and the air force. But she had
found that medicine very bitter and the transaction
less than honorable. She was determined at once to
make all the sacrifices necessary in order never
again to be exposed to such humiliation. In January, 1939, I went to Great Britain for a lecture tour
that took me into all corners of the country. There

I found out that public opinion was now ahead of the government. The latter was hesitating to adopt conscription; the country was energetically demanding it. Everywhere English men and women of all classes said to me:

"We must not allow this man Hitler to dominate Europe; we must have a large army and a strong air force."

When I returned to Paris I wrote an article in which I declared that England would institute conscription in March; at that time most of my French friends said I was crazy, that Great Britain would never impose obligatory military service in time of peace because one of her most ancient traditions was against it. But in the month of March, 1939, conscription was adopted.

The entrance of the Germans into Prague was a painful blow to Neville Chamberlain and to all those who, with him, had supported a policy of appeasement. The British Prime Minister was sincerely and profoundly shocked. He had determinedly hoped, in the face of all probability, that Hitler would never annex non-German peoples. Now he had proof to the contrary. He became suddenly (a fact of which many people are ignorant) one of Hitler's most determined opponents in England. It was under the influence of this emotion and this anger that he unexpectedly gave Poland a far-reaching guarantee. I was in America at that moment. Immediately I said to myself: "This means war." For it was certain, on the one hand, that Germany would continue her policy of expansion and would attack Poland, and on the other, that England would remain faithful, as she always has throughout her history, to her formal, written commitment.

This abrupt return of England to the field of European political cooperation led necessarily to a closer understanding with France. In June, 1939, the France-Great Britain Association gave a banquet in Paris at which were present Hore-Belisha, British Minister of War, Georges Bonnet, French Minister of Foreign Affairs and General Gamelin. On that occasion Hore-Belisha announced that in time of war the British armies would be under the orders of a French commander and that he was proud to be able to say "*our* General Gamelin." The latter remained impassive through prolonged applause. After the banquet we went with Hore-Belisha to the Polish Embassy, where a great ball was being given; he wished to show by his presence the new bond between England and Poland.

I retain a tragic memory of that occasion. It was a beautiful summer night. In the gardens of the Embassy the white marble sphinxes gleamed beneath the stars; an orchestra was playing Chopin waltzes and pots of red fire threw on the scene the glow of a conflagration. On the lawn beautiful women in crinolines (among them the two lovely daughters of the German Ambassador) were dancing with Polish and French officers. We all thought that the war was near, that Poland would be the first to be attacked and that this ball resembled the one given by Wellington in Brussels on the eve of Waterloo. Negligently sipping champagne, Ministers and Ambassadors discussed trifling subjects. There was talk of the maiden voyage of the Pasteur, and some of the persons present spoke of trips they were planning to South America.

A few days later Hore-Belisha returned, with Winston Churchill, for the review of July Fourteenth. It was a splendid occasion, Paris' last happy day. Never had the French Army been more magnificent. We had assembled in that parade everything that constituted our glory; the Chasseurs, the Zouaves, the Marines, the Foreign Legion and the Maginot Line Infantry. Winston Churchill beamed. "Thank God for the French Army," he said. We did not know at that time that the courage of men, their military virtues and the traditions of even the finest regiments are powerless when the mechanical equipment is not worthy of the army. The procession of tanks reassured the onlookers in the Champs Elysées and filled them with enthusiasm, but the latter were uninformed of the situation in Germany, they did not know that the Germans possessed many more tanks, more heavily armored and invulnerable to our anti-tank guns.

In the afternoon Hore-Belisha came to see us at Neuilly with a Colonel who was his aid-de-camp. He talked of the difficulties he was encountering in building up a British Army:

"Conscription," he said, "is all well and good, but for the moment it is more a formula than a reality. I cannot call up all the men who have registered because I have neither equipment to give them nor officers to train them."

"What about the officers from the last war?" I asked.

"They do not understand the new weapons."

"And if the war were to break out tomorrow, how many divisions could you send us?"

"Right away? Not more than six."

That figure frightened me. I was even more terrified when I learned a few weeks later that our General Staff had asked from England *for the whole duration* of a European war only thirty-two divisions. I remembered that in 1918 we had had as many as eighty-five British divisions, that the Americans, the Russians, the Italians and the Japanese were then our allies and that, nevertheless, we had won the war only by a hair's breadth. Here was cause for grave alarm.

Such was the opinion also of Georges Bonnet, who was at that time Minister of Foreign Affairs. I heard him recount the following incident:

"A few days before the war," he said, "toward the end of August, 1939, I called into my office two of the generals who were responsible for our army and our air force. I told them that we were drifting toward war and that, if Poland did not give in, war would be inevitable within a short period. 'Nevertheless,' I added, 'if you tell me that we have no serious chance of being victors, then I shall ask Poland to cede Danzig and the Corridor to the Germans. I know that in doing this I shall run grave risks. People will say that I have betrayed Poland after having betrayed Czechoslovakia. But that makes no difference to me. I prefer anything to the destruction of my country, which, moreover, would carry with it the destruction of Poland. Do not make the mistake of thinking that I have any illusions about the Germans' willingness to fight. Germany has been preparing for seven years for a European war and sooner or later she will start it, if she cannot win by simple threat of war the hegemony she desires. But it might be to our interest to delay the outbreak. It might be to our interest to gain six months or a year which we could devote to an intense effort at rearmament. That's why I turn to you and ask: "Are there pressing military reasons for demanding this sacrifice from Poland?" ' They answered me, each one separately, that they saw no military reason for postponing the outbreak of war and that a delay would be as useful to Germany as to ourselves. In these circumstances there was nothing more I could do."

Nevertheless he made a final effort. On the 31st of August, at one o'clock in the afternoon, François-Poncet, who had been appointed French Ambassador to Rome, telephoned him that Count Ciano had offered to call a conference to settle the Polish problem and also the other disputed claims. Georges Bonnet believed the sincerity of Count Ciano was above question: Italy was not ready to engage in a campaign; her treaty with Germany still allowed her three years' respite; Italian public opinion was averse to war; the last interview between Count Ciano and Mr. von Ribbentrop was said to have been less than cordial; Italy could obtain without fighting, in the course of a conference, a large part of what she desired. Such a conference, therefore, seemed as much in Italy's interest as in that of France and England. Bonnet determined to do everything in his power to support this project. He went, so he told me, to see Daladier, informed him of the Italian suggestion, and added:

"There is a meeting of the Cabinet at six o'clock this evening; I shall recommend the acceptance of the Italian proposal. I ask you to support me. In this way we shall present Germany with a *fait accompli*."

Daladier promised. But Bonnet knew only too well the character of the Premier, an honest man, but of such instability and lack of will, that he was constantly at the mercy of each new adviser. Bonnet was anxious all through the afternoon and he had good reason to be. For that evening, at the meeting of the Cabinet, Daladier did not support him. The Italian proposal was not definitely rejected, but the Cabinet expressed the desire first to see the direct negotiations between Poland and the Reich continued. The official communiqué, published at nine o'clock in the evening, said simply: "The Cabinet took a unanimous stand in support of France's commitments." On the first of September at dawn the German Army marched into Poland.

The next day at 2:15 P.M. Bonnet, who was in his office at the Quai d'Orsay, heard his telephone ring, picked up the instrument and was astounded to hear without any preliminaries:

"This is Count Ciano. I have in my office Mr. François-Poncet and Sir Percy Lorraine. I believe it is still possible to take up the subject of a conference. . . ."

Georges Bonnet promised Count Ciano not to

send a definite ultimatum to Germany until the next day, Sunday, at noon.

At this point there occurred a very strange episode which, I believe, has never been explained until now. It is known that France, in conformity with the promise given by Georges Bonnet, waited before sending her ultimatum until Sunday at noon and, before declaring war, until five o'clock. England, on the contrary, declared war on September third at eleven o'clock in the morning. Here is the reason for this strange procedure:

Contrary to the state of affairs at the time of Munich, English public opinion in 1939 was extremely hostile to the idea of a new capitulation. The Members of Parliament who had just had the opportunity during their vacations of talking with their constituents had been struck by the extraordinary determination of the whole population. Convinced that war was inevitable, the English masses thought it better to get it over with quickly. The Members of Parliament had been much impressed by this state of popular opinion and they were determined not to let Mr. Chamberlain show the same weakness as in the preceding summer. The result was that on the third of September at nine o'clock in the morning, Lord Halifax called Georges Bonnet by telephone and said to him:

"I am aware of the reasons that prevent you from sending your ultimatum before noon, but we have not made the same promises to Count Ciano and we are obliged to send ours this morning. The House of Commons convenes at noon and if the Prime Minister appears there without having fulfilled his promises to Poland he may be overthrown by a unanimous movement of indignation. . . ."

This is why two Allied nations declared war at an interval of six hours.

Thus on the third of September, 1939, a war began for which Germany had been preparing for a long time, for which England and France were absolutely unready and which Germany, with supreme adroitness, contrived to have France and England declare.

Today one can say that that war was lost, so far as France was concerned, at the very moment it was begun.

It was lost because we did not have enough airplanes, or enough tanks, or enough anti-aircraft guns and because we did not have enough factories to build what we lacked. It was lost because our Ally had only a tiny army and did not possess the means of expansion which would have permitted him to take quick advantage of his immense reserves of men and riches.

In the course of the conversation about which I spoke at the beginning of this article, Winston Churchill made use of an analogy that I found very striking. When I asked him why England, at the time of the Sanctions, had given in and allowed the Italians to have their way:

"Have you ever," he asked me, "observed the habits of lobsters?"

I replied that the habits of lobsters had never been one of my special hobbies.

"Well," he said, "if you have the opportunity, study them. They are very interesting. At certain periods in his life, the lobster loses his protective shell. At this moment of molting even the bravest crustacean retires into a crevice in the rock and there waits patiently until a new carapace has time to form. As soon as this new armor has grown strong, he sallies out of the crevice and becomes once more a fighter, lord of the seas. . . . England, through the fault of imprudent and cowardly ministers, has lost its carapace; we must wait in our crevice until the new one has had time to grow strong."

Circumstances, alas, were to lead France and England to sally out of their crevices, without a carapace, to do combat against the most terrible of enemies.

II

WHY THE FIRST EIGHT MONTHS OF THE WAR WERE WASTED

AT THE beginning of October, 1939, a short time after the first English troops arrived in France, I received a letter from the British Army Council inviting me to come to the General Head-quarters of that army as "French Official Eye-witness." My duties would be to follow the course of operations and to maintain contact between the British troops and the French people by such varied means as articles, lectures and talks on the radio.

During the four years of the last war I had been a liaison officer attached to the British army; I retained the pleasantest memories of my English and Scotch comrades; I had, in fact, written my first book about them, and so I was naturally tempted by this offer which was made with a great deal of warmth and cordiality. Being a reserve officer in the French army, I transmitted the letter to my superiors and at once received an order to accept. Thus it was that I went to Arras wearing a lieutenant's uniform (my rank in 1918) to present myself to Lord Gort, the Commander-in-Chief.

General Viscount Gort was staying at that time in the Château d'Habarcq near Arras. His aids-de-camp, a magnificent Scotch officer wearing a kilt with the Gordon tartan and having a beautiful silver-hilted dagger stuck in his be-ribboned stocking, and the amiable Lord Munster, descendent of William IV of England, received me there. In the small waiting room Gordon and Munster offered me a strange and violent cocktail which they called "the Habarcq Horror." Then they said: "Now we'll take you to the Chief."

Never has a generalissimo had a simpler office. A scrawled card, affixed to the door by four thumb tacks, read: "Office of the C-in-C." Inside the room, which contained no other furniture, two trestles of white wood supported a bare plank. This was Lord Gort's work table. The simplicity was intentional.

Lord Gort believed that a chief should live in the same way as his men. Extremely active by nature, he found, in time of war, his only sport and relaxation in walking. He was to be seen at dawn on the muddy roads around Arras, his elbows close to his body, his head thrust forward, his red and gold cap defying the rain, followed by a panting aid-de-camp.

Gordon told me that one day his chief had taken him to the Hotel Crillon for a conference with General Gamelin. He, Gordon, had been delighted at the thought of passing a pleasant evening in Paris. But after dinner Lord Gort had said:

"Now we'll go for a walk."

Whereupon, elbows close to his body and head thrust forward, he made three very quick turns around the Louvre, by way of the rue de Rivoli and the quays, and then went home to bed, still followed by the disconsolate Gordon.

The thing that struck me, on seeing Gort for the first time, was his air of youth, vigor and animation. Hore-Belisha had just rejuvenated the command of the British army. And he had been right in doing so.

Lord Gort spoke first of Hitler's plans:

"Will he attack through Belgium? I think he will," said the general, "because it is the only operation possible. You remember Foch's dictum: 'In war you do what you can, making use of what you have.' Only I don't see how Hitler can launch an offensive in winter in this Flanders mud, and if several months are to pass without fighting I'm afraid our men will become bored. It's no joke, you know, when darkness comes at four o'clock, to go back to a damp barn with no light but a candle."

"But, sir, in 1914 we spent all our time in dugouts and trenches."

"That was different," he said, "at that time we had an enemy in front of us who saw to it that we had enough to do. Here I am holding a line in front of Lille and Douai." (He got up abruptly to show me the line on the map.) "I have nothing in front of me except Belgium, a neutral country. It's not easy in these circumstances to maintain a fighting spirit. No, if this inaction is prolonged, a way will have to be found to distract the men. Lord Nuffield has offered me radio sets, but that's a problem in itself. Our soldiers can't use radios that require an outside source of current because they have no electricity in their cantonments. And so we must have radios that work from storage batteries. But then the batteries will have to be recharged. I'm engaged at the moment in having some cars equipped to go from unit to unit to perform this service."

He described the fortified lines that, according to information he had received from his Intelligence Service, the Germans had constructed in Poland against the Russians. This was at the time when people still hoped that these two nations would not long remain on friendly terms—a tenacious illusion, like so many others. Then he talked to me about the work I was to do.

"I want you," he said, "to talk to my men a great deal about the French army and to the French soldiers about our army. Then, too, we must make opportunities for our regiments to meet each other. Yesterday my lancers had lunch with your cuirassiers. That's fine. I myself often see General Giraud, Commander of your Seventh Army, stationed on my left. He's a splendid soldier."

The cigarette he had given me was starting to burn my fingers and I looked about for an ashtray.

"Oh, throw it on the floor," the general said.

For, as a matter of principle, Lord Gort, who discarded all useless objects when on a campaign, did not own an ashtray.

Next day I began my inspection of the front lines. These lines, as General Gort had said, had nothing opposite them except customs barriers and Belgian policemen, but they might, if Germany invaded Belgium, become from one day to the next the scene of the great battle. I was *horrified* at their weakness.

I had known, to be sure, from hearing it often repeated, that the Maginot Line ended in the neighborhood of Montmédy, but I naïvely believed that it was prolonged along the Belgian frontier by a series of fortifications that were perhaps less strong but nevertheless formidable. I received one of the greatest and most painful shocks of my life when I saw the pathetic line which, on a part of that frontier, was all that separated us from invasion and defeat.

What was to be seen in front of Lille in the month of October, 1939? Here and there, at a distance of one or two kilometers from one another, were little

concrete casemates surrounded by barbed-wire entanglements. Each of these casemates was occupied
by a British detachment; five or six men under the
command of a corporal or sergeant. Each contained
a periscope for observing the terrain, a machine
gun and a Bren gun (light machine gun). In addition each *was supposed* to contain an anti-tank gun,
but only the emplacements were there. The guns
were to come later.

Between the casemates extended an anti-tank
ditch, not very deep and half caved in. A little farther back the English soldiers were at work digging
trenches and dugouts. But in the deep mud of
Flanders, at this time of year, the work was hopeless. As soon as these unfortunates had dug down a
few feet into the yellow earth they encountered
water. They performed miracles of ingenuity in an
attempt to drain these inexhaustible wells, they installed elevated duckboards and parapets supported by sod. The results were not encouraging.
The English war correspondents, almost all of
whom had, like me, taken part in the campaign of
1914-1918, looked at these trenches with a critical eye.

"If that's our line," they said, "God help us! The means of attack are ten times more powerful than in 1914 and the means of defense ten times weaker!"

These honest journalists were made extremely unhappy by the severe censorship which forced them to hide their anxieties and reassure the public.

The officers of the regiments that occupied this line did their best to take a less pessimistic view. One of them, showing me a miserable trench which his men were digging with great difficulty, said in an apologetic tone:

"Obviously this would never stop a tank. But, after all, there's a thick forest in front of my battalion and it's reasonable to hope the tanks won't come this way."

During the following weeks, however, French and British engineers undertook extensive defense measures. Behind the front line of blockhouses many gangs of workmen toiled energetically in the construction of other concrete works. Almost anywhere you looked in the fields you could see the long iron skeletons that outlined future casemates, while, nearby, specialists in cement, who had come from England, were mixing sand and gravel. On the French sector, especially in front of Maubeuge, the new casemates had been admirably camouflaged. Many of them had the innocent appearance of houses or sheds. They filled the High Command with great confidence.

At this time many members of the French army were reading a book by General Chauvineau entitled "Is Invasion Still Possible?" This general, a professor at the War College, had reached the conclusion that concrete pillboxes rendered an invasion absolutely out of the question. "Works of this sort," he wrote, "can be built so rapidly that, in the time necessary for an enemy to take a first line, the defending army can construct a second. . . ." He had left two things out of consideration: first, that there might exist new means for attacking concrete forts; second, that a breach would permit the enemy to get behind the concrete line. In fact, that line at which our troops labored so painfully all through the winter in the cold and rain was never attacked from in front.

Most of the experts, moreover, did not believe, with General Gort, that there would be an attack against Belgium. "Why," they asked in their articles, "should Germany add to her enemies the Belgian army, which today is large and well-equipped?" Since, on the other hand, they maintained that the Maginot Line could not be forced, "there remain for Hitler," they added, "only two possible theaters of attack: Holland and Rumania, but it is highly improbable that he will choose either of these since Rotterdam is Germany's *last lung* and since Rumania is already delivering to the Reich all its surplus gasoline. . . ." Their conclusion was that Germany would do nothing this summer, that the situation was very favorable because "time works for us," that in 1941 "we shall have control of the air and, in 1942, enough heavy artillery and tanks to attack the Siegfried Line." These were sentiments that could be heard in those days in any mess at the front at dinner time; I often expressed them myself.

Hitler had said, referring to us: "I shall disintegrate their war," and in the course of this long winter of inaction he succeeded in doing it. The men got tired of digging trenches in the rain to defend themselves against an enemy they never saw. The divisions could and should have been taken out, one after another into the field, and given intensive training for an entirely new and terrifying kind of war. All the lessons of the Polish campaign should have been put to use. But we were so little war-minded that the generals allowed themselves to be stopped by scruples that would have been laudable in time of peace. I remember asking one of them why he did not accustom his men to the sight of flame-throwing tanks and dive bombers.

"If their first experience of this method of attack takes place on the field of battle," I said, "they will be terrified. If, however, they become accustomed to such sights the novelty of the impression will wear off."

"You are perfectly right," he replied. "I asked about it on several occasions. But I was met with the response that tank maneuvers would ruin the crops and that the civil authorities were opposed."

No one behind the lines seemed to be thinking about the danger of an enemy attack; everyone talked only about the danger of boredom. At the beginning of the war the men had lacked blankets, jerseys and shoes, and agencies to supply them had been established: Bundles for the Army, Cigarettes for the Army. Soon the soldiers were receiving too many packages, too many presents.

"With the best will in the world," an English soldier solemnly assured me, "I *cannot* smoke two hundred cigarettes a day!"

At that time prominent people in Paris and London had started a variety of new enterprises: Books for the Armies, Radios for the Armies, Amusements for the Armies, Burlesque for the Armies, Sport for the Armies, Art for the Armies, Plays for the Armies. A witty woman, disturbed at this frivolity, said that she was going to found a new agency— War for the Armies. She was right; but such ideas were not popular.

At the British front "Concert Parties," composed of famous comedians and beautiful showgirls, traveled about in military automobiles solemnly escorted by officers. Maurice Chevalier sang with great amiability for the troops of both countries. His arrival at Arras created more excitement than that of President Lebrun. He was acclaimed by the French and English soldiers. "Maurice, *'Valentine!'* " cried the French. "Maurice, *'The Rain Drop!'* " roared the English. When he left the stage he was besieged by autograph hunters: "Maurice, it's for my kids. I'm a papa, you know." At the door Chevalier turned around and said to the soldiers: "God bless you, boys."

It was all very pleasant, and harmless enough, but it was hardly an effective preparation for the German offensive. At a time when the country, in the gravest moment of its history, had only a few weeks at its disposal to make up for its past mistakes, to complete its fortifications and train its men, Frenchmen and Englishmen continued to live (except in certain sectors of the front) routine lives governed by the petty rules of a military bureaucracy.

In the city of Arras, where I was stationed, there were several thousand French territorials, old soldiers who had been mobilized—I never really knew why—and of whom the army made no use whatever. Their officers employed them as best they could to plant kitchen gardens, start poultry yards and raise rabbits and pigs. These were praiseworthy enterprises but it might, perhaps, have been more useful to fortify Arras and the line of the River Scarpe. A commandant, one of my friends, dared say as much to his general. The suggestion was not well received.

"Fortify la Scarpe! But the enemy will never advance that far. You are a defeatist! Wait for orders!"

After one or two experiences of this kind, even the most zealous leaders went back to their routine. The soldiers, well-nourished and with little to do, got fat. The Tommies, as soon as night fell, set to work writing interminable letters to their wives and sweethearts; the officers were unable, except with great effort, to censor this monstrous correspondence. An unhappy captain would no sooner see his table cleared of one pile of envelopes before another and larger one would descend upon him. The petty quarrels of everyday life, nursed and brooded over, occupied the attention of men who should have borne in mind that the future of liberty and the destiny of the world depended on their ability as soldiers and their power of resistance. Hitler, as he had said he would, had disintegrated our war.

He was not able, however, to make it disintegrate completely. There were plateaus of heroism raised high above the general level of mediocrity, and these never allowed themselves to be submerged in the pettiness of daily life. Toward the end of December, I spent several days in the Maginot Line and returned full of enthusiasm. Not only had this chain of magic mountains, bristling with guns and impermeable to gas, given me (perhaps wrongly) a tremendous impression of solidity but I also admired the men who garrisoned the fortress.

Almost all of them were from Lorraine and had been recruited in the very region where their fort was built. This allowed them, even in time of peace, to go there every Sunday. I met young lieutenants, lawyers and engineers from Metz, who for eight years had spent every week-end in the Maginot Line, calculating artillery ranges. These painstaking labors assured absolute precision of fire. The spotters in front of the forts had before them photographs of the country divided into numbered squares. Perceiving the enemy in square 248-B, all they would have had to do was murmur "248-B" into the telephone and ten seconds later the occupied zone would have been deluged with shells and bullets.

The confidence of these young men in their armament and their devotion to the Crew (for each fort thought of itself as a ship) seemed to me an ideal of what all our armies should have been. I do not regret the enthusiasm I expressed at that time nor the praise I bestowed on the garrisons of the fortress. I still think the character and patriotism of these young men were worthy of admiration. When, later on, the Maginot Line was so rapidly taken it was *not* through fault of these crews. It was taken because it was turned. This disaster puts in question the wisdom of the statesmen who paid out, in order to build an incomplete and vulnerable line, sums of money that would have been enough to equip a formidable field army; but it detracts nothing from the ardor and the honor of the fighting men.

Christmas Day, 1939, I spent in Lorraine with the French and British troops, amidst scenery that would have brought joy to the heart of Dickens. No English countryside could have presented a more perfect Christmas setting. A white mist swathed the landscape and clothed it in mystery. One could hardly see for more than fifty yards, but each narrow circle of vision was a fairyland. Every tree and frost-covered bush was a cluster of glittering coral. Even the barbed wire, like some monstrosity touched by one of Shakespeare's fairies, was decked for the moment with the silver tinsel that glistens on the branches of a Christmas Tree. In the evacuated villages the snow had brought the dead houses back to life. Two laurels in front of an empty inn, powdered with luminous crystal, were like sprigs of diamonds. Each garden bush became a cradle, every forest glade a church of white marble. On the roads, French and English soldiers, invigorated by the cold, slithered over the thin coating of ice and exchanged joyful greetings. Then, as one drew near the front line, the silence became intense. No gun spoke, no voice or cry broke the enchantment. In the deserted farms no dog barked, no cattle lowed. The mist, masking the opposing lines, enclosed each outpost, each watcher, in a silvery bubble, adorned with sparkling branches. Indeed, this war-time Christmas may well have been, for some French and British soldiers, if not the happiest at least one of the most beautiful of their lives.

At many other points in the line, especially

among the motorized divisions of the cavalry corps, so well commanded by General Prioux, I found admirable troops. I remember, for example, the review of a regiment of motorized dragoons. What fine soldiers! Their step was vigorous, their heads snapped to the left an instant before they came abreast of the general, their eyes, fixed on his, were young and ardent; their heels thudded on the ground at the salute. In truth, the Grenadier Guards could not have done better.

But some of the more thoughtful French commanders told me disquieting things. One evening the general of a North African division admitted to me that he hoped for a negotiated peace.

"The Germans," he said, "greatly outnumber us and they have incomparably better equipment. The struggle will be most unequal. My men are as brave as any others but if they have no anti-tank guns they won't be able to stop armored divisions with their bare hands."

In March, 1940, I spent two days at the headquarters of General Giraud, who was one of the best French commanders. General Giraud had a

fine reputation in the French army. There were
stories of his escape through Belgium from Germany, how in various disguises he worked at different trades and finally got back to our lines. In
Morocco, he was thought to be endowed with the
baraka, a kind of lucky charm, but his boldness
frightened his superiors. Headquarters were always
a little afraid of his overreaching his objectives.
For the coming battle, the task in Flanders with
which G.H.Q. had entrusted him seemed made for
his particular temperament. His army formed the
mobile wing and was to make a dash as far as Breda
if the Germans entered Belgium. I had often seen
him in Paris, and later at the Front, very tall,
dressed in a long, light, close-fitting tunic; but I
had never had an opportunity of speaking to him
except formally. So I looked forward eagerly to the
days I was to spend with him.

I was not disappointed. Many military men are
careful, too careful, in conversation. Even their
most moderate opinions are prefixed with all sorts
of timid qualifications. What Giraud thought he
said straight from the shoulder.

"In war," he said, "you've got to take risks. Rea-

[45]

sonable risks, of course. Contrary to what people will undoubtedly have told you, I am no daredevil —far from it. But I believe in considered boldness. You remember Magin's attack on the German flank at Villers-Cotterets in July, 1918. I was told to make preparations for the division, of which I was Chief of the Staff, to go into action. We had to combine surprise with solidity. There was only one way to do that and it was to group all our tanks together on a very narrow front. With the division massed at the rate of one tank every ten yards, the danger was that it might have been annihilated by a bombardment. But the probability of such a bombardment was slight, since on the previous evening the enemy could have known nothing. A legitimate risk therefore, and I took it. My heart beat fast that morning. We were to attack at 4:35 a.m. I never stopped looking at my watch from three o'clock onwards. At 4:30 not a gun had been heard. I began to breathe more easily. . . . 4:31 . . . 4:32 . . . 4:33 . . . 4:34 . . . 4:35. With a terrific din the division moved off and I breathed a long sigh of relief. . . . The *baraka* hadn't let me down!"

Then he told another story when we had been

talking about the English, for whose character he expressed great admiration but whose slowness he found disturbing.

"In war," he said, "speed of action is everything. In a Moroccan campaign, I had to attack a tribe which lived in a well-nigh inaccessible eagle's nest on the top of a mountain. I sent for the C.O. of the Engineers and said: 'You see that steep wall? Good. . . . I give you three days to cut a road in it that will take motor transport as far as the summit.' He replied politely, but firmly, 'Sir, it's quite impossible. A job like that would take three months, not three days.' 'Very well,' I said, 'if it's impossible you needn't do it. I'll do it myself.' I sent for a Colonel of the Legion and drew up a plan for the road. I asked him to put on the job every man of his own and the nearby regiments, day and night, and I told him it had to be finished in three days. . . . And so it was done . . . and I attacked an enemy who didn't expect me and couldn't have expected me and who was beaten without striking a blow. The moral of which is that the best element of surprise *is to do the thing that seems impossible and do it quickly.*"

Naturally, I asked General Giraud about our

chances in this war. Even he thought we should not be in a position to attack before 1941.

"It's a most regrettable fact," he said, "but we're short of everything. . . . Aircraft! Do you know how many airplanes I, the Commander of an Army, have at my disposal? Eight. Just eight! Of course there's the Royal Air Force, which is excellent, but if I want it to make a reconnaissance flight for me I have to ask General Georges, who asks General Gamelin, who asks Marshal Barratt, who asks Vice-Marshal Blount, who finally orders the flight, but by that time it is often too late to be of any use."

"And what if the Germans take the initiative and go into Belgium?"

"Then we'll have to start fighting this year, but it will go hard with us."

Going back to Lille in his car, he talked about his sons, about their education and the dangers that beset characters in nations that are too rich and too happy.

How was the eight-months respite that Germany allowed us made use of in our factories? Very badly. And there were several reasons for this.

TRAGEDY IN FRANCE

The first was the stupidity with which the Commissariat directed industrial mobilization. Skilled workmen, who were indispensable for the manufacture of airplanes or cannons, were sent to provincial barracks where they swept out courtyards or peeled potatoes. It took weeks or months to locate them again and send them back to their machines. As a result, the Renault Factories, which in peace time employ more than 30,000 workers and which should have filled a place of immense importance in the manufacture of tanks and trucks, were reduced, at the outbreak of the war, to a personnel of from six to eight thousand men. It was fantastic.

The second reason: Because the engineers and financiers persisted in conducting this war as though it had been the war of 1914, all plans were made for a campaign of four or five years. As a result factories were built which would not attain their period of production until 1941 or even 1942. Instead of making immediate use, as best they could, of the existing plants in France, machine tools of the latest design were ordered in the United States, a country from which we should have ordered tanks and airplane engines. For the same reason the dollars and the gold possessed by England and France were carefully rationed. This treasure was divided into four or five parts, each one apportioned to one year. Great American factories, which could have produced *in time* the equipment necessary for our armies, remained without orders from the Allies. "Engines built in France cost us less," people said. They were destined to cost us the war.

The third reason: The programs were designed for a war which was never to take place. The General Staff determined upon a long-term preparation for attack upon the Siegfried Line. It had calculated, with admirable precision, how many heavy guns would be necessary for this operation, and these guns were ordered at a time when all our efforts should have been devoted to urgent and immediate needs—anti-tank guns, anti-aircraft guns and light arms, such as machine guns and submachine guns. Our patrols along the Sarre begged their officers to give them sub-machine guns, such as were carried by all the German patrols. There were none to be had. When the Germans began to drop parachutists, all officers were ordered to carry revolvers. But there weren't any more revolvers in France. I, myself, went to gunsmiths in several cities, including Paris, without being able to buy one. Finally, *at the beginning of June,* they were ordered in Italy! That was a little late.

The fourth reason: Finally, failure of morale, and political dissension hindered production. From the time that Russia aligned herself on the side of Germany, the numerous Communist workmen, without showing open opposition, worked languidly and with no enthusiasm. The almost complete suppression of profits discouraged the small employer. During this war one never saw, as one had in 1914, small workshops and garages busy turning out shells. For many months France worked at a peace-time tempo.

In October, 1939, Paul Reynaud, who was at that time Minister of Finance, decided one evening after dinner to make a tour of certain armament factories in the region of Paris. He was astounded to find them closed. They did not work at night. Next day he went to see Daladier:

"Do you know," he said half jokingly, "if we go on this way, we are going to lose the war?"

The idea seemed incredible to him, as it did to all of us at that time. It was, alas, only too true.

Everything went much better in the field of Armament as soon as this Ministry was put in charge of Raoul Dautry, an excellent engineer who had reorganized the railways of France after the War of 1914. But he was appointed too late. It was in 1936 that he should have been given the task of building a war machine. Dautry was, like me, a friend of Marshal Lyautey and I had a high regard for him. He was an energetic little man, firmly planted on his legs, and he had a habit of half-closing his left eye in conversation and shrewdly measuring his interlocutor. He had always been consistently successful in the many posts that had been entrusted to him and when he was asked his secret he would say: "I have a trick—work."

At the Ministry of Armament, which was installed in the Hotel Majestic, Dautry would be busy at dawn covering sheets of red paper with urgent orders for his departmental heads. When the latter arrived, they would find on their desks these red notes from the boss, to which a reply had to be forthcoming the same day. Brief, brusque and sometimes brutal, these red notes of Dautry were famous. Here are a few of them:

"*To all directors:* I observe that arrivals at the Ministry are late and departures early. I shall institute a system for keeping check of this."

"*To Monsieur A:* I know that the weather is fine; I realize it is hot. But I know, too, that we are at war and I do not wish to have Major X smoking his cigar at the window and enjoying the air."

"*To Monsieur B:* When men are available—which may happen at any time—they are to be employed in cleaning up, keeping order, picking up scrap iron, clearing out ditches or surfacing roads. No one is ever to be left without employment. It is a director's business to direct."

"*To a Manufacturer:* It is imperative that all French machines should run twenty-four hours a day. This is difficult but necessary. All the rest is a matter of detail, in which I am not concerned. I need everything and need it at once. *The purpose:*

To achieve victory as quickly as possible. *The means:* Perform the impossible."

Such was the law of Raoul Dautry and it is certain that if there had been a human being capable of actually putting France to work, he was the man. But when I talked to him alone, I found this man who was ordinarily so full of energy and confidence disturbed and pessimistic.

"When will you be able to give the armies everything they need?" I asked him.

"Everything? Not before 1942," he replied. "We have begun too late."

He was one of those who worked courageously until the end, but he could not perform miracles and Germany had several years head-start.

In January I was sent to England, by my French chiefs, to study the British war effort on the spot. My hosts took me aboard their men-of-war in the North Sea; they showed me their aviation schools, training camps for the army and factories for making guns and airplanes. Everything the Admiralty was doing seemed excellent. The air force, too, appeared admirable, though too small in numbers.

As for the army, even the French Military Mission itself could not obtain any information about the number of soldiers in training. I said to the English general who received me at the War Office:

"You tell me, sir, that the active army, the reserves and the territorials comprise about 750,000 men and that an additional 600,000 recruits have been called. Good. But then how does it happen that you have not already thirty or forty divisions?"

"Well, you see, this is not my job," he replied. "And the colonel who is in charge of effectives is not here today."

That evening in Parliament I met Hore-Belisha, who had just given up the Ministry of War.

"What do you think of our new conscript army?" he asked me.

"It seems to me," I replied, "to be made up of excellent material. But I am like Oliver Twist: *I ask for more.*"

As a matter of fact, aside from the Canadian Division, no one could show us a corps of troops larger than a battalion in training. The infantry was instructed by elderly sergeant-majors who taught them how to fence with a bayonet. This wasn't going to be of much value to them in the course of the campaign! At the tank school, the instruction was ingenious, but the tanks were superannuated and scarce. Everywhere I found good will, good humor, patience and an unbelievable assurance of victory.

While I was in England, I attended a session of the House of Commons. The subject of debate was austere enough. The Opposition wanted the Government to include in the War Cabinet a minister whose special province should be economic questions. The Government's reply was that the presence of Sir John Simon, the Chancellor of the Exchequer was enough. One would hardly have imagined that this would be an occasion for amiable and amusing exchanges. But such was the case. Herbert Morrison and Major Atlee, speaking on behalf of the Opposition, were courteous and gently ironical. Sir John Simon, who was defending himself, thanked them for it. Their urbanity, he said, brought to his mind a quotation from Isaac Walton's "Complete Angler"—"Treat your worm as if you loved it."

An Opposition member then rose to make an

amendment. "I believe," he said, "that I know the 'Compleat Angler' by heart: the text does not say: 'Treat your worm as if you loved it' but 'Treat your fish as if you loved it.' " Sir John spoke again: "The Hon. Member is right," he said, "but I thought 'your worm' might be more amusing." The House agreed with him. Whereupon he added that it was very difficult for him to take part in a debate of that nature. It reminded him of the time when the Lord Chancellor was presiding over the Privy Council and the order of the day was "Is an orthodox Englishman obliged to believe in eternal punishment?" A celebrated theologian objected. "It is unfair," he said, "that the Lord Chancellor should have the deciding vote on the question before us today, since he is himself too evidently interested in the result."

The Prime Minister, who was stretched out on a bench beside Sir John Simon, laughed heartily, and the whole House found pleasure in Sir John's wit and the Premier's amusement. Evidently Members of the House of Commons thought a certain gay detachment necessary to their mental health.

When I returned to Arras in February, 1940,

the head of General Gort's staff gave a brilliant
lecture:

"I consider," he told us, "that in the course of
these winter months we have won a definite victory. Just compare the situation as it was at the end
of August, 1939, with what it is today. At the end
of August, 1939, we believed we would have to
fight not only Germany but Italy, Spain and
Japan; we did not know whether America would
lift its embargo on arms; whether the Dominions
would be with us; whether the Arabs might not
take the field against us. And what do you see
today? Italy, Spain and Japan are to all intents and
purposes neutral; America has lifted the arms embargo; the Dominions are with us; even the Arabs
are giving us their support. If you add to this the
fact that French mobilization has taken place without disturbances and that a Blitzkrieg on the West-
ern Front appears now impossible, it seems to me
no exaggeration to say that we have gained a great
victory."

At that time these arguments seemed to me irre-
futable. But such was not the opinion of those who

could look into both camps. In the neutral countries, people no longer believed in our success. It is certain, for example, that Italy, which at the outbreak of the war had observed operations with a certain impartiality (although Mussolini had an obvious preference for Germany), came to the conclusion in February that the Allies had made bad use of the winter months and that the disproportion between our forces and those of the Reich, far from growing less, was increasing. The woman who used to give soothing talks in French over the Italian radio suddenly began to sneer and then became openly hostile. Those of my friends who chanced to encounter Italians reported sinister predictions.

"I say goodby to you," Count Volpi remarked to Pierre Lyautey. "You can form no idea of the torrent of fire and steel that will descend upon you. You will be submerged!"

At this moment Italy's decision was made and she was only waiting for a favorable instant.

What had taken place? Had we completely squandered those eight months of respite? To say yes, without qualification, would be unjust to the troops along the Sarre, who had fought to the best of their ability; to the French and English soldiers who had dug so much earth and mixed so much concrete; to the members of the general staffs who had prepared with such pains the plans they had been asked to work out. No, many Frenchmen and Englishmen, between September and May, had been hard at work, but a great part of their effort was wasted in useless tasks. Those who had directed them had been controlled by three false ideas:

1. That a line could be held, as it had been in 1914, and that consequently the essential thing was to build one and reinforce it.

2. That the experience of Poland was not applicable to France, and that consequently it was useless to re-train and re-equip our armies according to new principles.

3. That the war would be a long one and consequently it was necessary to make industrial and financial preparations for campaigns in 1941 and 1942.

If you add to this jumble of errors a general lack of enthusiasm which was caused, in France, by the political divisions of the country and in England by too much confident optimism, it becomes fairly easy to understand why France and England after eight or ten months of war were in no position to resist the Infernal Machine which the Reich had, for seven years, been constructing with such terrifying precision and unfailing attention to detail.

III

HOW THE CLASH OF PERSON-ALITIES IMPEDED THE CONDUCT OF THE WAR

VERY often in history the conflicts of rival leaders have interfered with the conduct of wars and with the government of nations. In 1918 France had the good fortune to find a leader energetic enough to restrain all those who might have tried to hinder his activities: that was Clemenceau. In 1939, on the contrary, during the whole campaign, Édouard Daladier and Paul Reynaud never ceased to contend with each other for political power, and their incurable animosity was one of the causes of our misfortunes.

On the day when King George VI was crowned in Westminster Abbey, a British officer who was sitting beside me turned to me, as Paul Reynaud made his entrance, and asked: "Who is that little man with the Japanese face?"

I replied: "That little man is the future Premier of France."

From the time when he married Jeanne Henri-Robert, daughter of a distinguished lawyer and childhood friend of my wife, I had followed Paul Reynaud's career with interest. I considered him one of the most intelligent of our politicians and also one of the bravest. On many occasions I have seen him, against his own interests, defend ideas that were anathema to his constituents. He alone had the courage, at the time when the pound declined, to advise the devaluation of the franc, a measure that events rendered inevitable later on. He alone among our statesmen made a careful study of the ideas of Colonel de Gaulle on the subject of motorized armies and carried on a campaign for the creation of powerful armored divisions. He alone at a time when the youth of France was abandoned to its own devices gave as a title to a political book: "Youth, What Sort of France Do You Want?"

A short time before the war he accepted the Ministry of Finance in circumstances that had led his predecessors to despair of France's credit, and he succeeded in a few weeks in bringing billions of francs in gold into the Treasury. I liked to see him, when a subject fired his imagination, get to his feet, put his hands in his pockets, throw back his head to raise his short figure to its full height, and hold forth in picturesque and biting phrases in a voice like quick hammer blows. "A little fighting cock," we used to say, and we hoped he would fight for the right causes.

But that combative intelligence, that slightly arrogant assurance, that harsh and brilliant logic and that air of always being right on financial and economic questions, about which the person to whom he was talking knew little, were designed to exasperate many politicians and in particular Daladier.

The latter was no less eloquent than Reynaud but his style was not the triumphant, aggressive and technical one of his rival; his was a familiar style, touched with sorrowful emotion. When Daladier talked to the French people about the war, small tradesmen, workers, peasants, everyone, felt that

this homely tone, these grave accents and this heart-
felt love of peace made the Premier a fellow to all
Frenchmen.

Edouard Daladier had been a professor of history and he had found in the history of France, as
well as in his own honest heart, reasons for a sincere devotion to his country. All this was admirable, but these qualities were vitiated by two grave
faults: a distrustful touchiness that made him sus-
picious of all his colleagues and a lack of will that
became at times almost pathological. He was subject at moments to terrific fits of rage during which
he would pound on the council table. His colleagues asserted that his fist sounded hollow. "A
hand of velvet in a glove of iron," they used to say.
But Daladier's true character was unknown to the
general public who saw only his vigorous thick-set
exterior, called him "the little bull of La Ca-
margue," and expected bold action from him.

"Who would be the ideal man to replace Daladier?" I asked Reynaud one day.

"Daladier as the French people imagine him to
be," he replied.

Edouard Daladier's irascible distrustfulness had

already embroiled him with Edouard Herriot, and the Radical Party had been torn by the War of the Two Edouards. In one of Tristan Bernard's comedies there is a character who is called by his friends Triplepaw and who is so uncertain about his own desires that on the day of his marriage he hesitates to go to the church. "Daladier is Triplepaw," Paul Reynaud used to say, and this Triplepaw side of his character explains, perhaps, why this radical minister became successively the creator of The Popular Front and the hope of the conservative bourgeoisie. Daladier, for his part, used to say of Paul Reynaud: "As soon as he starts to talk, he has such an air of self-satisfaction that, in order to stand him at all, I have to picture him strutting about with a peacock's tail."

Such were the two men whose duty it should have been to work as a team and to cooperate in governing France, then engaged in the most terrible of wars. In actuality, each irritated the other, and this mutual exasperation grew to hatred when the schemes of women further poisoned their relations.

TRAGEDY IN FRANCE

I should have preferred not to talk about this aspect, at first glance so trivial, of the frightful tragedy of which France was the victim. But, on the one hand, the essential facts today are known to all, and, on the other, it is certain that the private lives of some of our statesmen impaired their public usefulness. It would be wrong, very wrong, to say that the French way of life in 1939 was corrupt; millions of families in France led simple and united lives. But this was not true of the three thousand persons in Paris who, as Byron said, "because they go to bed late believe they are the leaders of the world." Most of these attached no great importance to their sentimental or sensual intrigues; but events were destined to prove that these intrigues could nevertheless place nations in jeopardy and that "the man who would be king" must first of all discipline himself and be the master of his own passions.

Daladier, after the death of his wife, had for his Egeria the Marquise de C. This gracious and beautiful woman, blond and youthful in appearance, had a taste for power and an unfortunate passion for economic and political doctrines. But she knew how to keep herself in the background, she never tried to show off her great man to the world and her discreet influence was not, on the whole, very harmful. On the other hand, Paul Reynaud's friend, the Countess de P., was slightly mad, excitable, meddlesome and, as the course of events was to show, dangerous.

One day when I had criticized in Reynaud's presence a particularly unsuitable political appointment made by Daladier:

"It was not his choice," Reynaud said, "it was *hers.*"

"That is no excuse," I said.

He sighed.

"Ah," said he, "you do not know what a man who has been hard at work all day will put up with to make sure of an evening's peace."

I felt sure Balzac would have made note of that sentence.

From the very start of the war the dominant characteristic of Madame de P.'s seemed to be ambition. It was not enough for her that Paul Reynaud was Minister of Finance; she was determined at all costs to make him Premier. She filled the salons of Paris with accounts of Daladier's lack of energy, and gave everyone to understand that it was urgent that Reynaud should succeed him. Naturally these remarks were repeated the same evening to Daladier and the latter's detestation of Paul Reynaud grew constantly stronger. There was a time when these two men, both members of the war Cabinet, were on such bad terms that they no longer spoke to each other. This was an absurd and monstrous situation, and fraught with danger for the country.

For my own part, living with the armies as I did, I liked nothing better than to see Paul Reynaud when I passed through Paris. He could inform me better than anyone else, in his brilliant and uncompromising fashion, about the political situation. It was thus that on the nineteenth of March, 1940, between two meetings of the Chamber of Deputies he came to dine with me alone. The day had been a bad one for the Daladier Cabinet. The defeat of Finland had exasperated Parliament, and Daladier was criticized for not having acted fast enough. Probably the criticism was unfair, for it would have been difficult, perhaps impossible, to organize an expedition of this sort, and it would likely have terminated in disaster. But the deputies had demanded a secret meeting which had taken up the whole afternoon and was to reconvene the same evening at ten o'clock.

"That poor fellow Daladier has had a bad day," Reynaud told us when he arrived at eight o'clock. "I should not be surprised if he were overthrown tonight."

"And who will succeed him?" my wife asked. "You?"

"That depends," Reynaud said, "upon the President of the Republic and also upon the elements that defeat Daladier."

"If you are chosen," I said, "you will have to secure Daladier's support. He still has great popularity in the country."

"That is because the country does not know him."

"Possibly so, but it is a fact. You have great talent, but you have no party. The Radicals will be faithful to Daladier, and the Right, to which you belong, also prefers Daladier because you despise the Right and take no trouble to conceal the fact."

He smiled and said he would try, if the President summoned him, to arrange matters so that

Daladier would retain the Ministry of War. At ten o'clock he left for the Palais-Bourbon. That night, as he had expected, Daladier was overthrown. President Lebrun called upon Reynaud, who agreed, without demur, to form a new cabinet. But in that difficult task this remarkably intelligent man gave evidence of amazing ignorance of public opinion and an equally amazing lack of intuition. It was then for the first time that I began to fear that, brilliant dialectician though he was, he might be cut off from contact from the real world. He lived among ideas, not among men. His ministry was so constituted that it necessarily united against him both the Radicals and the Moderates. True, he obtained the support of Daladier, but of a hostile and embittered Daladier who was determined, if he had the chance, to wreck the ministerial ship upon which he was far more prisoner than pilot.

When he appeared before Parliament Reynaud secured with the greatest difficulty a majority of *one* vote! Parliament did not like him and, at bottom, it was sorry for having overthrown Daladier. Feeling this air of hostility, Reynaud lost his customary self-assurance and made a miserable speech.

Next day I returned to my post in Arras where

I found all my French comrades profoundly shocked at the composition of the Reynaud Ministry. It seemed to them a deliberate challenge to public opinion. In time of war it was a serious thing to discover so complete a break between the government and a large part of the nation. I had not seen Paul Reynaud since he accepted the Premiership. From Arras I sent him, in guise of congratulations, a sentence from Barrès: "In time of peace Parliament represents the nation; but in time of war it is the Army." And I added: "Do not lose touch with it."

From the start of the war Paul Reynaud had shown his hostility to General Gamelin. He criticized him for his inaction and maintained that the army did not have confidence in him. These were questions upon which I found it hard to form an opinion. It was true that in September, 1939, the General had not made a vigorous attack on the Siegfried Line but had confined himself to cautious operations in the Sarre. His adversaries asserted that this period, when a large part of the German forces was engaged in Poland, would have been the best possible one for a decisive at-

tack. To this the General replied that at the out-
set of the campaign we did not possess the material
equipment for taking the offensive and in particular we did not have the necessary airplanes and
heavy artillery. Without this equipment, such an
attack would have entailed crushing losses.

"I shall not begin the war," the General had
said, "by a Battle of Verdun."

And he amplified his statement thus: "France is
a nation with a low birthrate and it sustained
frightful losses in the last war. It would not have
strength to survive another blood-letting. The war
she has to fight now must be a scientific war in
which everything is so precisely foreseen that the
losses will be almost nothing."

I admit that at the time his attitude seemed to
me a wise one. It would have been foolhardy for a
layman to pass judgment on the military ability of
General Gamelin. He had been at Joffre's side during the Battle of the Marne and had been the first
to conceive the maneuver that brought us victory.
He had been an exemplary officer of the General
Staff and later, on the field of battle, an admirable
commander of a division.

When you met him for the first time you were

surprised by his inscrutability. His short, stiff mustache, his small eyes and thin-lipped mouth gave him an indecipherable aspect, which no spontaneous gesture served to clarify. He had neither the sparkling vivacity of Foch nor the massive geniality of Joffre. He spoke very seldom, and I have seen him in peacetime sit through a whole meal in absolute silence. But he was well-informed, courteous and modest. The officers of his general staff felt a strong personal affection for him. For my own part I always found him very kind. The first time he came to the headquarters of General Gort and saw me in uniform he said:

"What? Are you still a lieutenant at your age?"

"I have been a lieutenant since the end of the last war, *mon Général*."

"Twenty years without promotion!" he said, laughing. "That's too much. I shall have you made captain."

When he returned I was still a lieutenant. He was amazed.

"What has happened?" he asked Colonel Petibon. "I told you to telephone the War Ministry that André Maurois was to be appointed captain."

"I did so, *mon Général,*" the colonel replied. "But there is an obstacle. The regulations require two periods of training. Mr. Maurois has had only one."

Whereupon General Gamelin turned to General Gort.

"Everything is difficult," he said, "but I should have thought, nevertheless, that a commander-in-chief would not have had this much trouble in bestowing a captaincy!"

When I had been promoted, he wrote me a cordial note: "At last! But I hardly dare congratulate you at this late date . . ." and he invited me to come and see him at the Château de Vincennes where he had his General Headquarters. I retain a very clear memory of that luncheon, which took place in the vaulted hall of the fortress and at which were present, in addition to the General's own staff, General Noguès, who was in command of our troops in North Africa and Mr. Brugère, French Minister to Belgrade.

Official business dominated the conversation; General Noguès discussed the needs of his army and then Mr. Brugère talked of the orders for arms which Yugoslavia had placed in France and which had not been filled. To both men General Gamelin replied with precision, clarity and an exact knowledge of available resources which made the best possible impression. He questioned me about the Fifty-First British Division which was leaving for the Sarre. Then the conversation turned to the French Academy and its dictionary, and he said to me:

"What we need is a name for the soldiers in this war. Those of 1914 called themselves *Poilus*, but those of 1940 have not yet been christened."

Mr. Brugère asked whether he expected an attack soon.

"Yes," he said, "everything points to it. Our fliers and our secret agents see all the preparatory signs: massed artillery, ammunition depots and the evacuation of civilians. Of course it may be a ruse, but Goering made a speech yesterday in which he foretold important developments and his practice on such occasions has been to tell the truth. It seems probable that the great attack is imminent."

The calm with which he awaited this blow was

reassuring. You said to yourself: "This is Joffre with his imperturbable good health." But Paul Reynaud did not share this opinion.

"Why have two commanders-in-chief?" he asked. "If General Georges is commanding our armies, let General Gamelin confine himself to the role of Chief of the General Staff and the National Defense."

The antagonism between the Premier and the Generalissimo was not merely one between two personalities, but rather between two theories of war. From the beginning of the campaign Gamelin had been an advocate of defense and temporization; Reynaud hoped to become known as the man of offense and action.

"A general who remains on the defensive loses all his battles," he said.

Since he had become Premier by promising to conduct the war "with increasing vigor," he felt obliged to undertake large projects. The possibilities, however, were strictly limited. He commenced by insisting, from the time of his first trip to London, that the British Government should lay mine fields in the territorial waters of Norway. A little later he resurrected from the portfolios of the Ministry of Foreign Affairs a proposed agreement with England which exacted a promise on both sides that neither one would sign a separate peace, a plan to which Daladier had always refused to agree. Then he reopened the question of Belgium. Was it necessary to wait for an appeal from the Belgian Government before entering Belgium? Reynaud tried to force their hand.

"Are you with us or against us?" he asked the Belgian Ministers. "If you are with us, then let us hasten to cooperate in strengthening the defenses of our frontiers. If you are against us ——"

General Gamelin was outspoken in his opposition to this attitude, which he believed might result in throwing the twenty-five Belgian divisions into the enemy's camp. A violent scene took place between the two men. Reynaud would have replaced General Gamelin by General Georges as early as April if Daladier, who was still Minister of War, had not threatened to resign. This was a risk Reynaud dared not run. His personal position, however, seemed to grow stronger. The naval victory at Narvik made a great impression in France and

Reynaud, sponsor of the Norwegian project, de-
rived considerable prestige from it.

"The iron route has been definitely cut," he told
Parliament on the twentieth of April. And the Premier who a few days earlier had had only a single
vote majority obtained the unanimous support of
the Chamber. This seemed reassuring, but a sena-
tor whom I saw that evening told me with diabolic
glee that it meant nothing.

"You don't understand parliamentary by-play,"
he explained in a pitying tone. "There were adversaries of Reynaud who worked hard to make the
vote unanimous because unanimity is impersonal,
national, patriotic, whereas a strong majority
would have meant a personal success."

Next day I was received by Reynaud himself.
Striding up and down his office at the Quai d'Orsay
with his hands in his pockets, he talked to me in
ringing tones about the situation he had found upon
assuming power. It horrified me.

"The tanks," he said, "existed only on paper.
Disorder was so great that the cannon and machine
guns that the army need were lying idle in the storehouses. The Germans had two hundred divisions,

possibly two hundred and forty; we had barely one hundred. Daladier, through his inertia, thwarted all reforms and rendered government impossible."

"Nevertheless," I said, "Daladier is certainly a man who loves his country. He speaks of it so eloquently over the radio and in a way that goes straight to the heart."

"Yes," Reynaud said, "I believe he desires the victory of France, but he desires my defeat even more."

A terrible judgment; sincerely spoken but probably unfair, it reveals the depth of the abyss that separated these two men.

I saw Paul Reynaud once more on the sixth of May and found him depressed and nervous. On his desk were three telephones, one of which was connected with the Ministry, the second with the outside, the third with the room of Madame de P. This last instrument rang unceasingly. Reynaud would lift the receiver, listen for a second and then cry out in an exasperated tone:

"Yes . . . Yes, of course . . . But that's understood . . . But I implore you to let me do my work. . . ."

Finally he stopped answering.

The Norwegian affair went badly. It revealed for the first time the crushing superiority of the equipment at the disposal of the German army. It dampened the enthusiasm of even the most optimistic to observe the difference between minute preparation—an action rehearsed in advance down to its smallest details—and a hasty improvisation which exposed, to the bombs and machine guns of the enemy air force, soldiers who were courageous but ill-equipped, particularly in respect to anti-aircraft guns. Reynaud placed upon his enemies responsibility for this lack of preparation that led to disaster:

"They kept things from me," he said, "particularly a letter from Admiral Darlan which described the difficulties of the enterprise and which probably would have stopped me. But this afternoon I am going before a Committee of the Senate and I shall tell them the whole truth."

This time the quarrel between Daladier and Reynaud was so violent that President Lebrun had to interfere to reconcile them.

On the following day I went to the French Academy, which meets every Thursday. The Academy was, as usual, at work on the dictionary. The word *aiguiser* passed without comment, but *aiguiseur* was suppressed and the definition of the word *aile* led to a passage at arms between Abel Bonnard and Georges Duhamel. The previous edition had called a wing "a muscle."

"It's perfectly ridiculous," Bonnard said. "A wing isn't a muscle: it's a limb."

"On the contrary," said Dr. Duhamel, "a wing is a muscle. What you eat in the wing of a chicken is the muscle, no more and no less."

After a long discussion, it was agreed to insert a special remark on the expression *"aile de poulet."*

The contrast between the tragedy of events and this tender care for vocabulary may seem astounding, but I was glad to see the Academy carrying on its business despite everything. If everybody had done as much, things would have been different.

At nine o'clock on the morning of May tenth I was planning to go to the country to spend my leave there. At eight-thirty I switched on the radio and learned of the invasion of Belgium and Holland. The Great Offensive had been launched. All the officers on leave were recalled, and I went to the Gare du Nord to return to Arras. The train was so crowded with British and French soldiers that several cars had to be added. The state of mind of my many traveling companions appeared to me to be good. There was no anxiety but rather a certain satisfaction at being delivered from this long uncertainty. Wives had accompanied their husbands and were waiting on the platform for the train to leave. Standing near me by an open window in the corridor, an infantry captain was giving directions:

"Listen, my dear. Take the money out of the left-hand drawer of my bureau and the change that is in the drawer of the bedside table. The keys to the car and to the garage are in the tray on the chest of drawers in my room. Tell Berthe to put the business suit I took off in camphor. Have Jean's bicycle greased; it squeaks. . . . What did you say? That these two days have been very short? Certainly, but remember that we might not have had them at all. And if we stop those fellows, this may be the end of the war."

His little wife smiled bravely. It is *not* true to say that before the offensive the morale was bad. In the upper and better informed circles it may have been, but not among the masses who were still filled with hope and to whom the radio administered eight times a day their doses of illusion.

The news of the German break-through at Sedan was a terrible and completely unforeseen blow to the inhabitants of Paris. They were prepared, if need be, for the idea of a retreat; they had had experience enough of that in 1914. But they believed that any enemy advance would be quickly checked.

On the seventeenth of May General Gamelin advised the government that a German motorized column was advancing on Laon and that he could not answer for Paris longer than that night. That was a day of panic in the Ministries.

On the following morning the Parisians learned that the Germans had turned toward the sea and that they would have at least some days' respite. This time Reynaud, made bold by the gravity of the situation, took the action that he had so often postponed. In order to get rid of General Gamelin, whom he held responsible for the defeat and whom Daladier persisted in defending, he assumed for himself the portfolio of War and handed that of Foreign Affairs to Daladier.

Who was to be the generalissimo? For a long time Reynaud had had Georges in mind, but of all possible choices this would have been the most painful to Gamelin. For between these two men there existed a rivalry as persistent as that which divided Reynaud and Daladier.

"They are so busy making war on each other," an English General said one day, "that they have no time to make war on the Germans."

And it was a matter of great importance for the army and for the country that this transfer of powers should be accomplished amicably.

Another possible choice was Noguès who had had great success in Morocco and in all North Africa. Among the younger generals Huntziger and Giraud both had partisans. Huntziger was considered a man of great intelligence and his army had stubbornly resisted the attack. Giraud was a wonderful leader, but he terrified the timid by his audacity and, moreover, at the moment he was a prisoner. Reynaud decided upon General Weygand, who was in command of the Army of the Orient, and urgently recalled him to Paris. Weygand had been the second in command to Marshal

Foch at that moment in 1918 when the latter had taken command of a battle already half lost and transformed it into a victory. It was natural to make use of his experience.

At the same time Reynaud offered Marshal Pétain the Vice Premiership.

In the eyes of most Frenchmen the Marshal possessed incomparable prestige. His noble and regular features, tall stature, his somewhat cold and often satirical air of authority gave those who met him the impression of a "presence." Of the six marshals of the Great War, who had been the witnesses and artisans of glory, he alone remained with Marshal Franchet d'Esperey. And the fact that he bore so easily his eighty-four years and remained young inspired astonishment and respect.

In summoning Marshal Pétain to his side Reynaud thought first of all of strengthening his position and of stiffening and solidifying public opinion through this brilliant prestige. But he made a strange miscalculation in seeing in his new colleague only a name and a reputation. He was providing for himself a successor and a judge.

The disastrous struggle of Reynaud against Da-

ladier finally came to an end on the sixth of June
in the complete elimination of the latter. Master of
France a few months before and so powerful that
he had seemed to me untouchable, he disappeared
in the whirlwind that had struck his country without a single word of regret or even of surprise
being voiced.

Meanwhile General Gamelin, whom Daladier
had so long protected, was living between a courtyard and a garden, in the ground floor of a quiet
house on the Avenue Foch; dressed in civilian
clothes, he was spending his time tapping out on
his typewriter a memoir of self-justification.

A friend of the Gamelins, who had known them
in their days of power and remained faithful to
them in disgrace, went to see Madame Gamelin
just before leaving Paris. She found her calm and
resigned.

"The General," Madame Gamelin said, "is with
me. He is not thinking of himself but of France, of
our soldiers. He has the highest regard for General Weygand and hopes that he may succeed in
halting the enemy."

Then she pointed to the next room, where we
had, on a former occasion, admired a charming

portrait of the General, painted by his own mother when he was a child, and showing the young Maurice Gamelin wearing a long dress and beating on a drum, and her face took on the tender look of a loving and devoted wife.

"Do you hear him?" she said with emotion. "That's the clicking of his little typewriter."

These were the most serious of the personal conflicts that rendered the conduct of the war so difficult. It is easy to say that such antagonisms occur at all times, that jealousy and ambition are ever-present passions, that in 1914 Clemenceau and Poincaré hated each other and that nevertheless we were victorious. This is true, but in 1914 a certain nobility of heart and undivided patriotism triumphed over these passions. Poincaré had no love for Clemenceau but he loyally collaborated with him. Pétain, with self-abnegation, served under the orders of Foch. In 1940 France was so divided, political hatreds were so violent and the decline of public morality so far advanced that no obstacle was interposed to personal hatreds. The part played by personalities was not the essential cause of the defeat.

That cause, as we have shown, was lack of preparation, military, diplomatic and industrial, on the part of the Allies. But the quarrels of the Ministers and the lack of any leader capable of imposing unity on the nation deprived the armies of their last chance.

IV

WHY THE GERMAN OFFENSIVE
WAS SO QUICKLY SUCCESSFUL

A T THE beginning of May, 1940, I went to the
French front to visit the Ninth Army, the
one commanded by General Corap, which a few
days later was to break under the battering-ram
blows of the Panzer Divisions. The general staff of
that army was installed in the little village of Vervins, an old market town with sleepy streets and
half-closed shutters, whose rough cobblestones re-
sounded to the unhurried tread of military men
walking to their offices with the peaceful punctu-
ality of civil servants.

On the evening of my arrival I said in a letter to
my wife: "I have found good men here, but they
seem rather old and mossbacked. . . ."

[90]

TRAGEDY IN FRANCE

General Corap was a timid man, held in high esteem by his superiors, unmilitary in appearance, and running to fat around the middle. He had trouble getting into a car. His conversation was very interesting, but one felt his attention was directed wholly toward the past. He told me how, at the time of Fashoda, he had been mobilized against England as a young second lieutenant; and how in 1925 in Morocco he had captured the rebel Abd-el-Krim. This latter affair had been the peak of his career and, in the face of the task which now confronted the general, this peak seemed a mole-hill.

I visited the troops outside Fourmies and Charle-ville and was struck by their lack of numbers. Returning to Vervins, I had the feeling of traversing an abandoned country. As the car rolled from one ungarrisoned village to another I could not keep from thinking of an invading army. How little trouble it would have had, once the frontier was crossed, in advancing as far as Vervins! And what would it have found at the entrance to the town? Wooden barricades that a child could have knocked down, a sentinel with fixed bayonet and a

police officer. That was not much to stop an armored division.

The truth was that the general disposition of the
Franco-English troops did not meet the requirements of the new war as they had been made clear
in the Polish campaign, nor even the eternal requirements of any war.

How were our troops actually arranged? The
necessity of guarding a very long frontier had led
the High Command to establish a kind of thin ribbon from Dunkirk to Menton. This formation of
troops in a line was a survival of the war of 1914.
In that campaign it had been possible to maintain
it for a long time because the enemy did not have at
his disposal means sufficient to break our lines. But
it had been condemned as extremely dangerous by
all the great soldiers of history. They had been
unanimous in advising an arrangement *in depth*,
and above all the formation of a mass of mobile reserves, able, in case the enemy pierced the first line,
to counterattack or to close the breach.

But in 1940, because our effectives were miser-
ably inadequate, we possessed practically no body

of mobile reserves. Our best troops were along the frontier. If the enemy cracked that line the rest of the country would become scarcely more than a parade ground. No doubt he would encounter numerous towns on the way. But who would defend them? The idea of a frontal attack—advancing very slowly, a few kilometers a day at most, as in 1914, and quickly forming vulnerable salients—was so deeply embedded in everyone's mind that no one had even thought of worrying about the defense of Douai or Vervins, or Abbeville or Amiens.

The colonels and the generals in command of these places, close though they were to the front, were amiable old men who had long since been retired from active service and had been recalled at the outbreak of the war to be entrusted with posts that the army considered administrative sinecures. Never had these honest bureaucrats, submerged as they were under waves of papers, considered what they would do if enemy tanks or motorcyclists armed with machine guns should present themselves at the gates of their citadel.

This situation was all the more serious because these villages behind the front together with the railways that connected them constituted *the lines of communication* of our armies. The British army could be supplied by the railway line Amiens-Arras-Douai-Lille or at need by the line Abbeville-Boulogne. But if these lines were severed, that army would find itself completely cut off from its bases. Its storehouses of food, equipment, and munitions had been established at Le Havre, Chartres and Nantes; its advanced depots were in the region of Abbeville, Saint-Pol and Arras. What would happen to it if the enemy broke through the front and disrupted the communications between these depots and the armies? Clearly the latter, within a very few days, would be without food and shells. But what had the High Command done to ward off this danger? What steps had they taken to stop an attack that would come, not from the front, but from the side? Exactly none.

And even if it had been deliberately decided to stake the whole Allied cause on a single card, the front line, then this line should have been held at all costs. Although it was not very strong, it did exist. In March and April great excavating machines, brought over from England, had been in operation on the British front digging anti-tank ditches much more formidable than those whose inadequacy had alarmed me in October, 1939. But the action that seems the height of human folly, after spending eight months in building block-houses, was to abandon, at the first move of the enemy, all these fortifications, constructed at such great pains and expense, in order to engage in open country in the most hazardous of pitched battles.

"In this war the first one who comes out of his shell will be in great danger. . . ." It was General Gamelin whom I once heard make this statement. And so it seems probable that this fatal sortie was not according to his wishes, but rather was forced upon him by political considerations. It had certainly been prepared for a long time. For months I had seen the general staffs studying in detail "The Advance into Belgium" and carefully rearranging their marching orders in order to gain five minutes in their timetables on that day when the King of the Belgians should summon us. It had been calculated that the resistance of the Belgian army would give us time to occupy a line from Antwerp to Namur. General Giraud was to rush ahead as far as Breda. The Germans themselves knew exactly what our movements would be in the event they invaded Belgium, for we had been obliging enough to hold a rehearsal under their very eyes.

It happened this way. One day a German airplane landed in Belgium. This plane carried officers of the General Staff and a complete plan for the invasion of Belgium on a specified date. The German officers made a pretense of trying to burn their documents, but they were careful not to succeed. We were immediately informed, and the British army was put in State of Readiness No. 3, then No. 2, then No. 1—this last meaning that it must be prepared to march within two hours. Immense troop movements then took place, all the reserves advanced to the frontier, and the Germans, from the height of their reconnaisance planes, observed and recorded them, probably both delighted and amazed at the success of a stratagem that was at once so old and so palpable.

Naturally no invasion took place at this time, the Belgians did not summon us, and our divisions returned to their points of departure at the expense

of great quantities of gasoline. But General Mac-
Farlane, Director of Military Intelligence and a
man with a thorough knowledge of the German
army, who alone among all the English held wisely
pessimistic views about the issue of this campaign,
continued to consider an offensive against the Low
Countries a certainty.

"The hundred and ten German divisions are
still in the region of Aix-la-Chapelle," he said.
"They're not being kept there without reason."

On May 11th I entered Belgium with the British columns. In the charming little towns, with
their ancient houses, and in the well-kept villages,
women were standing on their doorsteps, with their
arms full of flowers offering them to the soldiers.
One of the British war correspondents who had described this truly triumphant entry with honest
lyricism was summoned back to reality by a tele-
gram from his paper: *"Less flowers, more facts,
please."* He had no trouble obeying that order.
From the second day the flowers disappeared and
facts made themselves brutally felt.

In the Belgian villages women still stood on

doorsteps, but they were looking anxiously at the sky. Nevertheless the German airplanes had thus far done little damage. Here and there, in a village, two or three houses had been destroyed. Elsewhere the Germans had aimed at a grade crossing and had hit the watchman's house. In the open country a few buildings were burning, among them a convent and its chapel. But none of this seemed very serious to me. I was wrong. We were naïvely rejoicing because the Germans did not bomb our columns. We said: "The German Air Force is not as strong as it was supposed to be." As a matter of fact they did not bomb us because they *wanted* us to advance as far as possible. Our advance served their strategical plans. The real purpose, at that stage of operations, of the German Air Force in Belgium was to terrify the civilian population and in this they were completely successful. Later on we discovered that in each village there had been a member of the Fifth Column, a German or Belgian, whose duty it was, as soon as the first bombs fell, to say to the inhabitants:

"Leave at once while there is still time! Soon this village will be destroyed, and the Gestapo will fol-

low the fliers. You know how they treated the
Poles!"

The people listened to them. The whole village,
infected with a strange collective panic, would
leave with its Mayor, its curé, its town officers. The
roads were flooded with refugees. It was an amazing spectacle. First came the cars of the rich, driven
by chauffeurs wearing gloves and smart caps; then
those of the middle class, driven by their own owners, with a mattress tied across the top; then the
big country carts drawn by horses and carrying
whole families; then platoons, battalions, armies
of bicyclists, to whom the red blankets tied to the
bicycle frames gave a brilliant color that would
have delighted a painter; finally came the heart-
rending procession of those afoot.

Nothing is more contagious than flight. As soon
as this tidal wave, which had formed near the
French frontier, reached a new town it caught it
up and carried it along with it. Our motorized columns, which had set out on the first day in such fine
formation, floundered in these waves of human
beings. British officers would considerately call a
halt in order not to run down mothers and children.

All troop movements became impossible. It has been asked why certain counter-attacks were not launched in time. In nine cases out of ten the choked roads are a sufficient answer.

Never in the war of 1914, even at the time of the break in the front before Amiens, did we see similar disorder. Why? Because now the terror was greater than in 1914, because stories of horror, no doubt spread deliberately, inspired all, even those who were passionately devoted to their lands, with a desire to escape from an undefined and dreadful danger; because the radio had spread alarming news among the masses of peasants who in 1914 had remained uninformed and hence inert; because the German Air Force possessed so great a numerical superiority that these unfortunates gained the impression that they were undefended.

To stop these people and force them to remain in their places would have required extreme firmness on the part of the civil and military authorities, absolute refusal to allow anyone to leave his home, and also some appearance of defense, a few machine guns mounted on the roofs, and a greater number of Allied fighting planes in the skies of

Belgium. But too often the authorities themselves were carried away by the tide; as for the machine guns and airplanes, there were none. Helplessly abandoned to their fears, everyone started off straight ahead without goal and without order. One would see ten thousand famished people suddenly descend upon a town like a cloud of locusts.

To this horrible confusion, which prevented the execution of orders, was added bad luck, which kept these orders from being issued in time. Not only were the Generalissimo and fifteen generals changed in the midst of the battle but General Weygand, who had to come from Syria, was delayed on his trip by a storm. The group of armies of the North that had received the brunt of the attack was commanded by General Billotte; at the most critical moment in the battle he was killed in an automobile collision. General Blanchard, who took his place, was, like him, an able leader, but he was taken by surprise without well-established communications with his troops and in most unfavorable circumstances for directing a battle.

Indeed, when one reflects upon the uninterrupted sequence of accidents, failures and fatal coincidences that alone made possible so complete and sudden a catastrophe, one cannot fail to be reminded of those classical tragedies in which Fate pursues, by the most improbable combination of events, an unfortunate hated by the gods.

I was with the British General Staff when the latter learned of the disaster at Sedan, the German break-through and the rout of Corap's army. For two days my English comrades—from delicacy, I think, and perhaps also from timidity—did not tell me about it. The official communiqués continued to be cautious and obscure, but I could easily see that something was being kept from me and I noticed that my friends stopped talking when I entered a room. Also orders for a retreat had been given. Finally the British told me what they knew.

The break-through had been immediate and complete. How had this been achieved? As a result of mass, surprise and terror. Thousands of tanks equipped with flame-throwers and airplanes equipped with sirens had been hurled upon Corap's army. No doubt we should not have believed it if, before the battle of Sedan, we had been told about screaming planes. It sounded like a novelist's, not a soldier's idea. Rudyard Kipling had made use of it in a curious anticipation: *As Easy As A B C*. But experience did prove that the combination of a screaming noise with a huge, white jet of flame, created a vision of Apocalypse. The bravest men, placed unexpectedly before such a menace, for which they had not been prepared, had little chance of holding their ground.

Even so they would have tried to resist if they had had guns capable of stopping tanks. One can imagine their horror when they discovered that their shells could not penetrate the armor of the most powerful German tanks. The Skoda works had built armor plate thicker than any that had been foreseen and these new tanks ignored our projectiles as Gulliver had ignored those of the Lilliputians. Our artillery men discovered fast enough that our seventy-fives, fired in certain circumstances, could serve at need as anti-tank guns; but this was an expedient and not an organized defense. Moreover German planes and tanks worked so well together that a battery had little chance against them.

All of us asked each other in the month of May: "How did they pass the Meuse? Hadn't the bridges been mined?" What was said then in the British army was that parachutists or spies had killed the men whose duty it was to blow up the bridges and that, moreover, the number of mines had been insufficient. In addition, the advance of the German motorized units had been so greatly aided in Ardennes by the Belgian Fifth Column that their speed greatly exceeded anything had had been foreseen and Corap's army was taken by surprise.

One of the most courageous actions of the war was performed over the Meuse. Certain French and English aviators received an order to destroy specified bridges at all costs. Two groups of bombers, one from each country, sacrificed themselves. The French went first at a low altitude, then the British followed. I never learned the number of French losses, but I know that of sixty British planes forty did not return.

This example, as well as a thousand others, proves that the most heroic courage was not lacking in the Allied armies. It is *not* true that the soldiers showed themselves from the beginning morally incapable of resistance. The soldiers of General Prioux, of General Fagalde, of General de la Laurencie, of General Janssen, were just as good as the best soldiers of 1914. The tanks, the French Cavalry Corps, the anti-tank crews, and also many of the British units behaved admirably. The defense of Dunkirk by Admiral Abrial was the equal of any of the great sieges of history. But German material superiority was such that heroism alone could not conquer, and just as microbes, which try without success to attack a healthy body, can easily permeate an organism already weakened by fatigue or worries, so the elements of moral weakness which existed in our armies suddenly began to multiply as soon as one dreadful experience had shown the insufficiency of our armament.

Victory and defeat are habits. Lieutenant de Jumilhac, who had acted as my guide when I visited Corap's army and who was a horseman, said to me while talking about the Norwegian Expedition:

"It's bad business that our first enterprise in this war met with failure. A young horse must never be defeated in his trial runs. If he is, he gets the habit, loses his self-respect and comes to consider it perfectly natural that he should stay behind."

What is true of horses is also true of armies. A victorious troop acquires a vital force which multiplies its strength; a vanquished troop loses its confidence.

After the disaster at Sedan the myth of the enemy's invincibility spread rapidly and served as an excuse for all those who wanted to retreat. Terrifying reports preceded the motorized columns and prepared the ground for them. These columns, veering toward the West, took our armies of the North from behind. Trying to elude them, the British General Staff to which I was attached took me with it toward Arras. The city was buzzing with rumors: "The Germans are at Douai . . . The Germans are at Cambrai . . ." All this was to be true a little later; at the moment it was false; but a phrase murmured from shop to shop, from house to house, was enough to set thousands of men, women and children in motion, and even to startle military leaders into ordering their detachments to retire toward the coast, where as it turned out they were captured.

TRAGEDY IN FRANCE

German parachutists in Holland and Belgium played a role that was real enough, but fear of them increased their effectiveness tenfold. In the eyes of the peasants and soldiers every costume became a disguise. No priest was considered a priest any more; an officer in uniform might prove to be a fake officer; authentic telephone messages were received with suspicion. Jean Cocteau, when I saw him a little later, told me with a poet's vivid conciseness: "All you see now on the roads of France are nuns winding on their puttees."

It was these myths and rumors, a hundred times speedier than Messerschmitts, that explain how such small forces were able to occupy important positions without a fight. A few motorcyclists, bold and well-armed, would enter a railway station, kill the employees and disrupt the train service. Often those in possession could and should have defended themselves. I encountered a group of British engineers who, with shovels and pickaxes, had killed one at a time all the members of an advance motorcycle detachment.

The defense of Arras by the Welsh Guards and by a handful of French Zouaves was another ex-

ample of what could be done in this war-behind-
the-lines by a group of resolute men. I saw the
Guards, aided by a French officer, Commandant
Poumier, prepare the defense of their positions
with great calm. At all the entrances to the city
they erected sandbag barricades which protected
machine guns and anti-tank guns. When the German tanks arrived, they stopped them by destroy-
ing some and setting fire to others. The enemy column made a detour around the city, but the city's
effective and courageous resistance continued for
almost a week, then the Guards and the Zouaves
retired in good order toward Dunkirk.

Such strong points, had there been enough of
them, would have made possible the counter-attack
that General Weygand had carefully planned and
that was designed to close up the breach from Arras
to Bapaume behind the German motorized columns. The disorder caused by the fugitives, the
lack of reserves, the disruption of lines of communication and the disorganization of the Allied general
staffs by the enemy air force, prevented it from ever
being launched. The speed with which information
was supplied by the German espionage service ap-

proached the miraculous. Hardly had a general established himself in some village when the enemy airplanes came to bomb him.

Blitzkrieg, as it had been described by the Italian General Douhet and as the Germans had waged it in Poland (a war we believed impossible against an army well established in its positions) had proved possible and victorious through the German superiority in equipment, the inadequate number of our effectives, our lack of depth and also through that imprudent, that mad advance into Belgium which rendered useless the network of subterranean communications established by our armies in the course of eight months.

Amiens was the parting of the ways for my English comrades and me. We had arrived there in a torrent of refugees. The whole city was full of them. Around the railroad station, seated on their bags, on sidewalks, on pavements, they made an immense human carpet worked in dull and lifeless colors. They had emptied the larders of the restaurants, the ovens of the bakeries, the shelves of the groceries, as completely as necrophagous insects clean out a corpse.

The charitable Salvation Army alone was able to give me a cup of tea. I went to sleep rolled up in a blanket.

At three in the morning, Colonel Medlicott, with whom I had gone there, sent me word that it was dangerous to remain in Amiens, that he was starting for Boulogne, and that he assigned me the duty of taking back to Paris with Lieutenant Klee all the French journalists attached to the British army, for whom to his great regret he no longer had means of transport.

This was an order that was easier to give than to carry out. The Germans were approaching and thousands of refugees besieged the station. Jostled women emitted shrieks. The only train that was still scheduled to leave for Paris carried as many as twenty persons in each compartment. Distracted mothers were handing babies through the window to travelers crowded on the seats, who had never seen the babies before, telling them: "You'll give him back to me in Paris . . ."

To find a place in any of these cars was hopeless. Finally an ingenious and intelligent military commissioner authorized us to get into the baggage car which was taking to safety the cash from the railroad stations and from various branches of the Bank of France.

Thus it was, standing between boxes filled with coins in a train pursued by German airplanes, that we returned to Paris. It took us fifteen hours to make a trip that in ordinary times takes barely two. At each grade crossing we were met by a flood of refugees, rising in sad, rose-colored waves. My journalist friends attracted attention by their uniforms (they were not the same as those of the army) and I heard people murmur: "Parachutists!" At one station a woman came to tell me they had found a spy disguised as an officer in the next car and that a policeman had shot him with his revolver. It was probably untrue but it gives an idea of the atmosphere of anguish and suspicion produced by this collapse.

Nevertheless the conductor of the baggage car, a solid old Frenchman, gray-haired and ruggedly built, maintained his equanimity:

"There is nothing I can do for you," he said to the refugees, extending his arms across the door of the car, "nothing at all! You cannot get in. This is a car containing cash. I have my orders to let no one on board and I shall let no one aboard. No, my dear woman, I am not heartless. Why did all of you leave home? Because a bomb fell on your village? Well, what of that? I saw plenty of bombs fall between '14 and '18 and torpedoes and artillery barrages, which are much worse. No one ran away because of them. What's that you say? That you're not soldiers? Oh, yes you are. In this war everyone is a soldier, since everyone is under attack. Don't you know you are helping the Germans by choking our roads, swamping the stations and slowing up the trains and the troops? At this moment there is only one thing that matters: to win the war."

The train went on very slowly. Above us German bombers, pursued by English fighter planes, tried to destroy the tracks. On an embankment some women, pointing first to the sky and then to the ground, joyfully indicated to us that one of the Germans had been shot down. I looked at the conductor who was disregarding all this noise and was quietly checking off his cash boxes. At that time I still had hope . . . However, when I saw the terrifying refugees all along the railroad from Amiens to Creil I received the impression of a cataclysm that nothing could stop.

I was exhausted when I arrived at the Gare du Nord but I had only one idea—to communicate as quickly as possible, to those who could make use of the information, the things my comrades and I had observed in the course of the retreat. It seemed to us that a small number of measures, relatively easy to adopt, would deprive the enemy of some of the opportunities he now had of successfully repeating the same operation.

I immediately composed a memorandum intended for Paul Reynaud, drawing his attention to the necessity of replacing the superannuated commanders in the towns directly behind the front by younger men who would be more resolute in defense; to the necessity of prohibiting civil populations from all movement; to the ways of defending cities against incendiary bombs and to other subjects of a like nature.

When I presented myself at the Ministry of War, Roland de Margerie, Reynaud's head diplomatic secretary and my friend, said to me: "Wait, you will see the Chief himself."

A little later, I was in fact taken into the office of the Premier and I handed him my memorandum. But I found him so completely submerged by the complaints that everyone was showering upon him that I had no illusion about any chance our modest suggestions might have of being acted upon. On that occasion Reynaud gave me the impression of a courageous boxer bravely trying to stay on his feet but already reeling and offering an easy target for a knockout blow. I stayed only a minute, but before I left I asked him, "Do you see any reason for hope?"

"As long as the patient is not dead," he replied, "the doctor always tells the family there's still a little hope."

He was standing in front of his desk, his head thrown back, his hands in his pockets. I have not seen him since that day.

I was received on the following day by my military superiors and I found them less pessimistic. They were loud in their praise of the disposition of the troops in depth along the lines of the Somme and the Aisne. General Weygand had decided, they told me, to make no attempt to form a continuous line but to allow the tanks if necessary to pass between the occupied positions and to hold the latter in order to prevent the infantry and artillery from following the tanks. Unfortunately we had lost our best divisions in the North and the new line was even thinner than that of the tenth of May.

On the third of June Paris was bombed by two hundred and forty airplanes. On that day Duff Cooper, the British Minister of Information, had come to Paris and I had been invited to lunch with him by two French ministers, Frossard and Jullien. This luncheon took place at the Ritz; at the moment when we were about to sit down at the table the sirens sounded an alarm. Immediately the waiters, according to regulation, disappeared into the cellars. The ministers and their assistants found themselves in an embarrassing situation. To seek shelter seemed to them to show lack of courage; to serve themselves lack of dignity. They took the course of sitting down at the table in front of empty plates and waiting to the accompaniment of a violent cannonade. But the alarm was a long one, and the greater their hunger became the duller grew the conversation. A secretary went to telephone the Prefect of Police and returned with the report:

"It's serious. Bombs have fallen on the Citroën
Works. The Ministry of Aviation is in flames.
There are several hundred casualties."

When I returned home, my children told me
they had seen the airplanes very high up like a
swarm of bees, flashing in the sunlight. Paris did
not seem at all terrified by this bombing. On that
occasion I came to the conclusion that the German
threat against London would not be as frightful
as people had thought. The following day news
came that the new German offensive had been
launched all along the fronts of the Somme and
the Aisne. As General Gort and his staff were no
longer in France, I made a request to join the
Royal Air Force, and permission was granted.

The General Headquarters of the Advanced
Striking Force was established at that time at
Troyes. I was received there by the Commander,
Vice Marshal of the Air Playfair. When one has
met a number of the leaders of the Royal Air Force
one is struck by a strange, indefinable similarity
among them. These handsome faces, with blue eyes
that remain young even under gray hair, this combination of gentleness and firmness, this friendly

but efficient discipline, are characteristic of the Army of the Air.

"Although the German Air Force is superior in numbers," Marshal Playfair told me, "it is certainly inferior to ours in quality. Their losses are three or four times higher than ours, so that today our situation is better than at the beginning of the battle."

But the French aviator, Saint-Exupéry, author of "Night Flight," whom I met a few days later, gave me a quite different report:

"The Royal Air Force," he told me, "is much too optimistic . . . For my part I am certain of one thing: my squadron has suffered terrible losses; very soon it will cease to exist."

I saw in the neighborhood of Troyes two fine squadrons of Hurricanes and some nineteen-year-old boys with blond hair and blue, forget-me-not eyes, each one of whom had to his credit more than ten victories, but I was struck by the small number of machines. The British had in France, at least in the region I visited, no more than a few squadrons left. When I returned to Paris (where I found a very sinister communiqué that talked of motorized

[117]

columns at Forges-les-Eaux and at the gates of Rouen) I communicated my impressions to my chief, Colonel Schiffer, and I added:

"I am sure the British still have a large number of fighter planes in England. We *must* get them to give them to us. It's their fate as well as ours that's being decided at this moment."

"You must go to London," he said, "and send out a sort of S O S to the English people by radio; apparently public opinion over there does not understand the desperate character of the situation."

"I shall be glad to go, *mon Colonel*. But I must have an order."

"I shall talk to G.H.Q. about it."

G.H.Q. sent Captain Hermant, with whom I had a conversation, and it was decided I should leave for London on the tenth of June in an army airplane. The news grew worse and worse. The German tanks had now arrived at Vernon, that is, at our gates.

For a long time we couldn't believe it, Paris was so quiet and beautiful. Every morning when I opened my window I could see the loveliest of pale blue skies, the trees of the Bois de Boulogne, the

Arc de Triomphe and the Fort of Mount Valérien looking in the mist like a Florentine convent. In the garden below, the *concierge* was watering the begonias of which she was justifiably proud. In the apartment underneath, a workman whistled a military tune as he mended a tap. Nothing had changed. It could not be true that the Germans were getting perilously near Paris.

On Sunday the ninth we began to read in the papers and to hear on the radio quite unexpected names of places. . . . Mantes . . . Pontoise . . . Was it possible the Germans were only half an hour from us by car, while we went on living and working just as usual? In the Champs Elysées, the terraces of the cafés were full. We had lunch in the open courtyard of one of the big hotels in the Place Vendôme. There were lots of people at the tables. The only sign of imminent departure was a large number of vans outside the Ministry of the Navy. Sailors were carrying out boxes and papers. We met the editor of a Paris newspaper and asked him whether this meant evacuation. He said the government was divided on the subject. We went to the cinema: it was nearly full. We saw the attack on

Narvik and the Paris raid. The tragedy of last week had already become entertainment.

On the tenth of June at seven in the morning, Roland de Margerie telephoned me that I had better send my wife south.

"Is the government leaving?"

"Today."

"But Paris will be defended?"

"No."

At that moment I knew everything was over. France, deprived of Paris, would become a body without a head. The war had been lost.

I was due at the Buc airport at noon. My wife and I decided to visit, perhaps for the last time, those corners of Paris we loved best. And so we said goodby to the Invalides and the Quays of the Seine and the Place Dauphine and Notre Dame. The city had never been more beautiful. The sky was pure blue, the air soft. In the streets, traffic policemen stopped our little car with as much punctiliousness as if the world were not about to come to an end. The salesgirls in the store we entered were alert and obliging. One sensed tears in everyone's eyes, but each went about his business without mentioning the great sorrow.

"The common people of France are magnificent," my wife said. "At once simple and brave. How can men like that have been defeated?"

"Men," I replied, "can do nothing against machines. They were ordered to defend a line. They would have defended it. But it was never attacked. It was taken from behind and encircled."

"I still can't believe," she said, "that the Germans are going to march into Paris. . . ."

A few days earlier we had had a long conversation about this entry of the German Army into Paris with one of our dearest friends, the surgeon Thierry de Martel.

"As for me," he had said to us, "my mind is made up: the moment I learn that they are in the city I shall kill myself."

And then he explained to us at length that most people do not know how to kill themselves, and bungle the job, but that a surgeon holds the revolver as precisely as he holds a scalpel and always hits a vital spot. Then, half-seriously, he added: "If you, too, have no desire to survive our misfortunes, I offer you my services. . . ."

At ten o'clock in the evening, when I was already on the plane bound for England, the sound of the telephone interrupted my wife, who was sadly selecting the few objects she could take with her. It was Thierry de Martel.

"I wanted to find out," he said, "whether you and your husband were still in Paris."

"André has been sent on a mission to London," she replied, "and, as for me, I am leaving tomorrow at dawn."

"I am going to leave too," he said in a strange tone, "but for a much longer voyage . . ."

My wife, remembering our conversation about suicide, understood that he was going to kill himself and attempted to dissuade him:

"You can still do so much good," she said. "Your patients, your assistants, your nurses, all of them need you . . ."

"I *cannot* go on living," Martel said. "My only son was killed in the last war. Until now I have tried to believe that he died to save France. And now here is France, lost in her turn. Everything I have lived for is going to disappear. I cannot go on."

And when she continued to plead with him he hung up.

On the twenty-fifth of June during a stopover of the clipper at the Azores, my wife, glancing over an American newspaper, learned that Thierry de Martel had killed himself by an injection of strychnine at the moment when the German army made its entrance into Paris.

In him we lost an incomparable friend and France one of the noblest types she has bred. This surgeon was a great gentleman. He had made fortunes and used them to support free clinics in which he operated on thousands of unfortunates. I know of a case in which he saved from death, by an operation that he alone could perform, a man who had pursued him for years with jealousy and hatred. He had proved on a thousand occasions his physical and moral courage. There is no better measure of the immense confusion of the French in the face of this complete disaster than the admission by this brave man that he was unable to go on living.

During the retreat from Flanders, on the road from Vimy, an old French peasant woman, standing on her doorstep and watching the procession of refugees stream by, said to me sadly:

"The pity of it, Captain! Such a great country. . . ."

The pity of it, I thought in my turn, when I learned of the death of Thierry de Martel. It was maddening to think that such people (for France had produced more than one) found themselves driven to despair, and a great civilization saw itself foredoomed, because five thousand tanks and ten thousand airplanes, which we could have built or bought without trouble, were not constructed in time.

V

HOW FRANCE AND ENGLAND WERE SEPARATED

FROM the beginning of the war in September, 1939, German propaganda set as its goal the separation of France from England. For eight months it pursued this aim with remarkable adroitness and tenacity.

Each day it repeated to the French that the English had dragged them into the war; that the English themselves were not fighting and, moreover, never had fought; that the English were furnishing the machines and the French the cannon fodder. It distributed pictures showing a bath of blood toward which an English soldier was pushing a French soldier, and others representing English officers in Paris fondling half-naked women while a French soldier kept watch in the Maginot Line. In June, 1940, it had succeeded not only in separating the two allied nations but in setting one against the other. Why this success?

First of all because this propaganda was reinforced in the minds of many Frenchmen by strong and ancient prejudices. Before Germany, and for longer than Germany, England had been France's hereditary enemy. The memory of nations is dreadfully retentive. In more than one French province, between 1919 and 1939, when I talked with confidence about British friendship, I encountered the vague, irritating and persistent memory of the Hundred Years War. True, Delcassé had reconciled the two countries in 1904 and established the Entente Cordiale; true, England had fought at our side with perfect loyalty from 1914 to 1918; true, there were a million British dead reposing in the cemeteries of Northern France; but after the war there had been new misunderstandings between the two nations. England, fearing France might grow too strong, had most imprudently favored the rearmament of Germany.

"We English," Lord Tyrrell, Ambassador to

France, said to me about 1930, "we English, after the war, made two mistakes: we believed the French, because they had been victorious, had become Germans, and we believed the Germans, through some mysterious transmutation, had become Englishmen."

In 1936 at the time when the German troops had reoccupied the Rhineland in defiance of the Treaty of Locarno, English public opinion, drunk with pacifism, had refused to support us.

"Why should we?" an English politician said to me. "The Germans can do what they like in their own back garden."

And another:

"What you hold against us English is that we are not good Frenchmen."

That was not true. What I held against some of the English at that time was that they were not good Englishmen and that they did not realize that a rearmed Germany, protected in the West by strong fortifications and animated by a spirit of revenge, would be as great a menace to them as to us.

For a long time I had felt esteem and friendship for the English people. I had served in the war of

1914 as a liaison officer with the British army. This experience had taught me that England carries out to the letter the agreements she has signed, though she seldom goes any further. I knew too that if she was capable, like all nations, of very harsh action when her national life was at stake, at least there was no malice in her violence.

It is inferiority complexes that make nations, like individuals, cruel. England had no inferiority complex. Far from it. Nine centuries of prosperity had instilled in her an invincible optimism. Because she had always ended by winning the wars in which she had engaged she had finally ceased even to think of the possibility of defeat and its terrible consequences. From the day of the Armistice England had wanted nothing but to return to her well-kept lawns, her country houses, her sports, her traditional way of life, and she turned a deaf ear to all talk of armaments and fighting. Her professors taught the youth of the country that war was a survival of barbarism and could easily be eliminated. They did not tell their pupils that unless force is used to sustain justice injustice will triumph.

In attaching so much importance to the idea of the League of Nations England was moved in part

by a sincere idealism but also by a false idea she had
formed of a League of Nations that would over-
come cannon with volleys of edifying discourse.
Harold Nicolson, a member of the British Parliament, told me he had received the following letter
from one of his constituents:

"I hope you are for the League of Nations *and*
no foreign entanglements."

This confusion of ideas, this incredible self-
confidence, this refusal to look reality in the face
had produced the effects that might have been foreseen. Having slumbered on her green lawns from
1919 to 1939 England awoke after Munich when
it was too late, and she came to the war with almost
no army.

That was the second element in the success of
German propaganda. "Just look," the French were
told, "the English have no soldiers; they will fight
to the last Frenchman." That was far from being
fair. England had the best Navy in the world and
an Air Force that gave promise of being *excellent*.
But it was true that on land, through lack of men
and arms, she could only hold a tiny sector of the
long line that ran from Dunkirk to Menton.

"The English? But where are the English?

There really are English soldiers in France?" many Frenchmen asked me ironically when I talked to them about the British army.

Even so, if Great Britain had acted promptly after the declaration of war, if she had quickly formed a number of new divisions, perhaps public opinion in France would have been reassured. But England, which is slow by nature and by principle, was never more so than in this war. The Trade Unions did not lift their restrictions on work for several months and until trade unionists had been admitted to the government. The business men were worried about keeping their export markets. Orders that should have been placed in America and Canada were not placed in sufficient quantity. The manufacture of airplanes did not proceed with real efficiency until that late day when it was entrusted to Lord Beaverbrook. In March, 1940, Raoul Dautry, French Minister of Armament, had been shocked to learn that the English experts were still wrangling over the type of tank they were going to put into mass production. About the same time General Billotte, commander of the group of Armies of the North, said to me:

"The English? They have, I know, splendid

qualities. They are soldiers that hold their ground well, and their leaders are men with experience in war, but they are maddeningly slow. Imagine, after eight months of war, they have ten divisions! With all the men they have conscripted they should have formed at least thirty! But they want to do things too well. They are finicky. The Germans, now, know the importance of the *time* factor. There are cases when it is better to have mediocre equipment in time than perfect equipment after the war."

The Chief of the Staff of the French Mission of Liaison, Colonel de Cardes, was also worried:

"I cannot secure precise information," he told me, "about the number of men the English are planning to send us in the course of the next few months. I need the figures in order to recruit my liaison officers. But no one seems to know. Sometimes they tell me four divisions between now and October; sometimes one. Sometimes they are going to form a second army, sometimes they decide not to. In any case we cannot count on anything of importance this summer. It's agonizing."

Nevertheless, despite prejudices and delays, German propaganda was far from having attained its

goal in April, 1940. To be sure one met plenty of
Anglophobes in France. There had always been
Anglophobes and, for some of them, it was a pro-
fession. But between the general staffs of the two
armies relations were good, better on the whole
than in 1914. The two admiralties had no secrets
from each other. The English told us of all their
most recent discoveries and we opened all our files
to them.

Fraternization between the troops was not easy.
Language constituted a barrier. But when occasion
presented itself the men showed good will toward
each other. I saw, for example, a Scotch battalion
give a bagpipe concert in the Maginot Line for the
fortress garrison. It was a great success. The bag-
pipes reminded the French peasants of the Breton
hornpipe, and two ancient civilizations became
friends. After the concert there was an exchange of
souvenirs; the garrison of the fortress had insignia
which they generously distributed; the Scots
opened their wallets and brought out photographs
of their fiancées or their wives. All this was very
cordial. Acute Anglophobia was to be found in the
ruling classes rather than among the people.

TRAGEDY IN FRANCE

It was the Navy and the Royal Air Force that saved the fighting prestige of England in the eyes of many French civilians. The episodes of the Graf Spee and the Altmark and the Battle of Narvik produced a great effect.

"All the same," even the most hostile of the French said when they heard these accounts, "those English are some boys!"

The Royal Air Force was very popular with us. At the beginning of the war, when France herself had so few airplanes, the exploits of the British Air Force reassured our soldiers. The latter loved to see a Hurricane surge up against the Heinkels or Dorniers and with a single burst of fire from its eight machine guns bring down an enemy plane in flames.

The English machines—both the Hurricane and Spitfire pursuits and later the Defiant as well as the Blenheim and Wellington bombers—were much admired by our experts. And the pilots were worthy of the planes. Enthusiastic young sportsmen, they were a delight to see in their blue-gray uniforms and they were as modest as they were brave.

"Is it hard to shoot down a German bomber?" I enquired one day from a boy of nineteen who already had several German planes to his credit.

"Hard?" he said. "No, it's not hard. All you have to do is to follow exactly the instructions given at the flying school. They told me there to follow the enemy plane, disregarding its fire, until it was about three hundred yards away, then to get it in the center of this little red circle that you see on my windshield. At that moment they said to press the button that controls all eight machine guns and the German would crash. I followed instructions. At three hundred yards I got the enemy machine in the center of my sights. I pressed the button and the German crashed. You see it's not hard."

But if the machines and pilots were perfect, the organization of the Royal Air Force was too complicated. General Gort had under his command in the North a certain number of planes which constituted what was known as the Component Air Force. In Champagne there was another group that was known as the Advanced Striking Force and was composed chiefly of bombers. Finally a large number of machines remained in England to defend the English factories and villages—the so-called Fighter Command.

A pursuit plane can stay in the air for about an hour and a half, and so the squadrons stationed in Great Britain could rarely be of service in France. They had fought at Dunkirk because the battle there was very close to the English coast. They arrived in a half hour from their English airfields, spent another half hour fighting, which permitted them to do good work and left them a half-hour's supply of gasoline to get back to their base. But the farther south the field of battle moved the less possible became this maneuver. It is this that explains the progressive diminution in numbers of the English squadrons engaged in the Battle of Flanders and the growing discontent of the French command.

The Battle of Flanders, like every defeat of a coalition, gave rise to mutual recriminations. Not that courage had been lacking. In the British Army, as in the French Army, many units conducted themselves admirably. But some explanation had to be found for the disaster.

"We were encircled," said the English, "and we lost our supplies and equipment because of an error in strategy which *we* did not commit."

"It is true," the French replied, "that mistakes have been made, but the first and most serious of them was not to have an adequate number of men and in that *you* bear a large share of the responsibility."

The first reaction of Winston Churchill after the engagement at Sedan was to minimize the seriousness of the defeat. Arriving in Paris, on the fifteenth of May, he astonished and revitalized the Supreme Council by the vigor of his determination. Those who saw him that day were filled with admiration at his rage, which was like that of an old lion, and at the power of his eloquence. He was opposed to the idea of a retreat from Belgium and the abandonment of Louvain and Brussels. He wanted to fight the offensive by a counter-offensive.

But on the twenty-sixth of May, Reynaud in his turn went to London where he made a discouraging report and said that unless the English were capable of making a massive effort France would be forced to abandon the struggle. Two days later on the twenty-eighth of May the defection of the Belgian Army precipitated the retreat to Dunkirk.

After Dunkirk there were eddies of public opinion in England. "Let us not send back to France," wrote certain journalists, "those divisions we have just saved at so great a cost. They will be useless to the French Army, whose situation is desperate, and they will be lost for the defense of the British Isles." Even those who did not share this insular egoism maintained that it would take at least three months to re-equip troops that had lost everything.

What remained in France to represent the British Army at the time of the Battle of the Somme? The Fifty-First Division had escaped the disaster of Flanders because it was in the Sarre. It was sent to the region of Saint-Valery-en-Caux. A motorized division which was in process of debarkation and a few units of a third division completed this tiny army. The Canadians crossed the Channel, but they arrived too late and re-embarked without fighting. Thus at the moment when the greatest battle of the war was being fought, against more than a hundred and fifty German divisions, there were in France barely three or four British divisions. For those who understood the circumstances, this perhaps was an inevitable consequence of the defeat in Flanders. But it is natural that the French Army should have had at that time the feeling of carrying the whole weight of the war alone.

"The English?" the German radio commented suavely. "They know only one military operation—re-embarkation. You will soon read in their newspapers triumphant communiqués announcing that His Majesty's Navy has achieved a great success in re-embarking the last British soldiers without disorder or bloodshed."

Appearances gave support to these propaganda talks. The English Generals, rendered distrustful by the Battle of Flanders, were afraid of being encircled and, on instinctive impulse, tried to get their backs to the sea. The French Command felt this uneasiness and feared its effects. The period of trustful collaboration was over.

At the beginning of June the state of mind in both armies seemed to me so disturbing that I emphatically called it to the attention of my superiors. It was then, as I have said, that I was assigned the mission of going to England to draw the attention, not of the government (which was well-informed) but of the English people, to the desperate situation in France; and to say that Great Britain, giving no thought to her personal security, must send us her last airplane and last battalion.

I left from Buc near Versailles in one of the Royal Air Force planes. The machine that was to take me, a Flamingo, was the one that had just that morning brought Lord Lloyd over to France. But when the mechanics tried to start it, one of the propellers refused to turn.

"This is how we win the war!" the pilot said angrily and we took another plane, less elegant but more tractable. The usual course by way of Boulogne and Calais had become too dangerous. We headed west, saw below us German columns marching across the Norman plain and left France in the neighborhood of Caen. I recognized the mouth of the River Dives and the beach at Cabourg on which I had played in my childhood. The crossing was a long one but without incident. In the plane Captain Crawshay told me about the death of Gordon, the handsome Scotsman whom I had admired at the headquarters of Lord Gort on that first day, and who had asked to resign his post at headquarters to assume command of a battalion of Gordon Highlanders.

It was a strange England, tiny and exquisite, that I discovered through the window of the Flamingo. Its winding roads, its pretty villages, its camps, its well-kept lawns on which traces of work could be seen so plainly from the skies, seemed to be part of some delightful exhibition of toys. One's heart tightened at the thought of other airmen seeing these same cottages, these camps, these oil tanks, and hurling their bombs on them.

From the Hendon airport I went straight to the French Mission who took me to the British Ministry of Information. In this building I found I had a great many friends: the minister, Duff Cooper; his parliamentary secretary, Harold Nicolson (one of the best writers of our time) ; Ronald Tree ; Lord Hood and a dozen others. I arrived at the exact moment when the daily press conference was meeting. Charles Peake of the Foreign Office, who was presiding, pushed me onto the platform and said:

"Since your mission is to make known the situation in France, this is your chance. You will be talking to the whole British press."

I did not know what I was going to say; I had not prepared anything and I am, in normal circumstances, completely unable to improvise in English. But on that day I was so moved by the misfortunes of France and by the frightful future opening before us, that the words gushed out. When I had finished, to my great surprise, the three hundred journalists who were present got up and applauded for a long time. I don't believe anyone until then had told them with equal frankness the hideousness of France's position, the necessity of immediate help and the impossibility of our holding out unless England had reinforcements to give us.

After this talk Nicolson and Peake took me to Duff Cooper. It was agreed with him that I should repeat that same evening, over the radio, what I had just said and that the British Broadcasting Company would give me its "best time," that is, the "Postscript to the News" at 9:15 P.M.

I hastily composed a message which ended thus:

"It is not in 1941, it is not this autumn, it is not even next month that our friends can help us: it is *now*. We know how magnificently the British Army and the Royal Air Force have fought, we know that they have done all that it was possible to do. The time has come to do what is impossible. We have complete trust in our British Allies. We know they are ready to throw into this fight all they possess. What we ask them to realize is the importance of *time*. Remember what we might call the Spirit of Dunkirk. Before Dunkirk it was thought impossible to evacuate in a few days, from a half-shattered harbor, more than 30,000 men. Wild optimists said 50,000. In fact, 335,000 were saved. How was it done? Who knows better than you do, you who have done it . . . And if you show once more the Spirit of Dunkirk you can also win this battle and the war . . . For Dunkirk you gave every ship. Give now every plane, every man, every gun. Let us together ask America, now so ready to help us, to produce in one or two months what under general conditions would take years. It is impossible, all experts will say, to equip, to train and to send over in a few weeks a large army. That is true.

It *is* impossible but it must be done, and it will be done . . ."

The British Broadcasting Company asked me to return at two o'clock in the morning to repeat the same message, this time in French, for the Province of Quebec and also to come back next day to talk to the English schools. I was in a state of extreme fatigue, not having slept for two nights, but I was happy to see how quickly the British public responded to my appeal. During the days that followed innumerable letters reached me. All expressed the same desire: "We want to help France. What can we do?" Here is one among a thousand. It came from a woman.

"Dear Mr. Maurois: Your appeal tonight, on the wireless, just went to my heart, and I am sure to the hearts of thousands of the Britons. It seems awful that one can do so little personally to help our brave Ally. I am going to put every penny I can screw on into Saving Certificates, to pay for men and munitions, and every day I am going to pray for France like we prayed at the time of Dunkirk. Don't let France ever despair, as we will never let her down. Is there any Fund which receives

gifts to turn into money for France? If so, I have
a small silver tea set which I would be very happy
to give. I hope your broadcast will bring an enormous amount of help and sympathy . . ."

The things that struck me were the desire to help,
an abandoned generosity, and a profound ignorance
of what this war really was. When I described the
suffering of the refugees, the bombing of villages
and of Paris, and the martyrdom of our armies,
facts which I believed known to all, I noted with
surprise that people listened to me as though I were
a being from some other planet.

The following incident may give some idea of
this state of mind. Since I had received my instructions quite unexpectedly and, moreover, had lost
everything at Arras and Amiens, I arrived in London without any other belongings than a kit-bag
with two shirts and a sponge-bag in it. . . . My
country was invaded. I had no idea where my wife
and children were. I was worried almost to despair.
The first English friend I called on realised my distress despite my endeavors to conceal it. Always
sympathetic and understanding, he immediately

made up his mind to be even nicer to me than usual. He asked me to dinner and then, with a great effort, said:

"You needn't change. . . ."

Which, considering that all I possessed in the world was a uniform, made me smile despite my troubles.

I heard another significant story from a naval officer. His destroyer had sunk a German ship and taken its captain aboard. The German was a devout Catholic and, as it seemed to the British officers, a man worthy of respect. They treated him very well indeed. Then, as the commander of the destroyer was spending the night on the bridge, he offered his cabin, the best on the ship, to the German. But down below the German stopped short on the threshold of the cabin and backed away:

"No," he said. "This is a trap of some sort."

"Why?"

"Because it's quite impossible that you'd be giving your Commander's cabin to a prisoner."

"But why? You're our guest."

And then, convinced they were in earnest, he

stood and looked at them for a long time in silence. Then his eyes filled with tears and he said:

"Ah, you poor lads. You've no idea what you're fighting against."

After my broadcasts many young men came to see me.

"It's a shame," they said to me, "that we haven't been called up yet! Can we enlist in the French Army? We'll do it right away."

I got the impression that public opinion in England wanted the government to take stronger measures. But good will is no substitute for tanks or planes or rifles.

"These letters and visits," I said to my Army friends, "are touching. But actually *what* can you give us?"

Their faces became grave and distressed.

"Aside from the Canadian Division which has just left," they replied, "we have no troops equipped for a war on the continent. We haven't supplies to replace all we lost in Flanders. We shall certainly send several squadrons of airplanes, but it is essential in our common interests that our aviation factories and our ports should remain defended. If you can hold out until 1941 . . ."

Then I knew the game was lost and there was no more hope for France.

I said to the French Ambassador, Charles Corbin, whose attitude through all this difficult period had been both courageous and high-minded:

"After all, it *is* strange that in the tenth month of the war the English have no army!"

"Yes," he replied, "but we must be fair. They have kept to the letter the agreements they made. The dates were fixed for the formation of the British Divisions; these dates have been met. The fault, our fault, was not to have demanded of our Allies as many divisions as in 1914, but it is a fact that we did not ask them for anything of the sort. The myth about the power of defense and about fortified lines blinded our general staff and our ministers."

On the morning of the thirteenth the newspapers announced the Germans were in front of Paris. As I was sadly reading the *Times* I was called to the telephone, and a lady-in-waiting informed me that the Queen wished to see me at eleven o'clock in

Buckingham Palace. I had been presented to Queen Elizabeth when she was Duchess of York; I had seen her again, as Queen, in Paris, but I did not know to what I owed the honor of this audience. The Palace with its tall footmen dressed in red, its innumerable commemorative pictures and its bamboo furniture, still appeared very Victorian. Sir Alexander Hardinge conducted me to the Queen.

"Mr. Maurois," she said, "I wish to tell you that I feel great sorrow for Paris . . . and great sympathy for the French in their misfortune . . . I love France *so much*. During our trip to Paris two years ago I felt the hearts of the women of France beating so close to mine. I am going to try to talk to them this evening over the radio and to tell them the simple truths that come straight from my heart."

She talked to me about this broadcast and then asked me about what I had seen, and about my wife and children. I told her I had no news of them. Her soft eyes expressed so much human compassion that I was profoundly moved. When she had said, "I love France *so much*," I had felt that this was no official phrase but a cry brought forth by true emotion. The Queen, like her people, wanted to do everything to aid us. But it was too late.

After the fall of Paris Winston Churchill went to Tours where he was horrified by the complete disorganization of the country. The airport at which he landed was deserted. No members of the government, no representative, came to meet him. The city was overcrowded with refugees and he had great difficulty in finding the government of France.

There, in a chateau on the Loire, the French Premier told him that he, Reynaud, stood for continuing the struggle but that he might be forced to make way for another government which would ask for an armistice. In that case what would England say? Winston Churchill was not able to release France from her promise not to make a separate peace, but the British Cabinet, I believe, let it be understood that there would be no vain recriminations and that the restoration of France to full independence would remain one of its war aims. This meeting between Reynaud and Churchill in Touraine was the last.

On the 27th of June I went to Wiltshire to see

Sir Eric Phipps, former English Ambassador to France, and he invited me to listen to a French broadcast with him. The battle cry from the Marseillaise: "Citizens, to arms!" brought tears to my eyes. It was then that I learned of the resignation of Paul Reynaud and the request for an armistice. I owe it to truth to say that my English friends, in these circumstances that were so painful both for them and for me, conducted themselves with a decency and a generosity worthy of their noblest traditions. They recognized at once that the mistakes in this lamentable adventure had been made by both sides and that reproaches were useless. Sir Edward Grigg, Under Secretary of State at the War Office, sent for me:

"I simply want to tell you," he said, "that we understand and that we do not blame you. We have not been able to help you in time; you could not act otherwise."

Then he talked to me about the fleet. It was *the* one thing that worried all the English. In the days that followed the atmosphere became more stormy. The conditions of the Armistice caused grave alarm. It was said that at Bordeaux the English Ambassador, Sir Ronald Campbell, was no longer being informed of anything. Lord Lloyd and General Spears, sent to take part in the discussions, were said to have met with no better luck. In London Corbin handed in his resignation saying he was unable to be the representative of a policy contrary to the one he had so long defended. Roger Cambon, who took his place, was not long in following his example and retiring in his turn. After him Boni de Castellane acted as chargé d'affaires with perfect tact and courtesy. France was very lucky in the men who represented her in London in such difficult circumstances. But what could they do?

At the last moment Winston Churchill had thought he could persuade the Reynaud cabinet to continue the fight by offering to unite the two empires under a single government presided over by a Frenchman. Every citizen of either country would have a double, Franco-British nationality. All resources would be held in common. It was an amazing offer and, had it been made a few weeks earlier, it would without a doubt have changed the course of the war. But it came at a moment when France was exhausted and wanted nothing but *immediate* succor: airplanes, tanks and cannon.

I have been told that General Weygand, in the

course of this discussion, recalled an episode from the life of Winston Churchill. The latter, during the war in the Transvaal, had been captured as he was getting out of a train by two Boers who pointed their revolvers at him.

"If at that moment," General Weygand was supposed to have said, "someone in the train had said to Mr. Churchill: 'Resist them! At home I have immense resources. I shall put them at your disposal,' this offer would not have altered the situation. Such today is the case of France; guns are pointed at her heart; she is disarmed. She can only do what Mr. Churchill did: accept destiny."

I do not know whether this account is true; but, be that as it may, the analogy is exact. Winston Churchill, however, who believed he had made France a prodigious offer—so great a one that several members of Parliament criticized him for having made it—was sadly wounded to see his proposal of union received with indifference. Many Englishmen shared his regret, and the best friends of France were perhaps the bitterest because they had been the most enthusiastic.

"What a shame!" the great English critic Des-

mond MacCarthy said to me. "I would have been
so happy to become a French citizen."

With him and with Raymond Mortimer, another
very talented writer, I spent a melancholy but
charming evening, the first for a long time during
which I was able to rise above the terrible events
of our time and talk of eternal things. It was a discussion such as must have been held sometimes in
the fourth or fifth century, in the Gallo-Roman villages under the heel of the invaders, by the readers
of Virgil and Horace. We talked about French
poetry, which my hosts knew so well. We recited
the verses of Mallarmé and Valéry and also those
of Malherbe and Racine. Then Desmond said:

"We know that we are menaced by many things:
first of all by death, which is not very important,
but also by tyranny, and that is more serious. Our
duty is to save a thing that can be saved and that
depends only on us: the confidence we have in one
another. To do that, two things are necessary: first,
that we shall never forget the existence of our
friends, their kindness and affection. Even if we do
not see them for long years; even when the French
are told that we English are monsters and when

[153]

we are told that the French have betrayed us, let us remember certain Frenchmen and certain Englishmen who, we know, are incapable of any but noble and generous thoughts. And when we have the opportunity let us be very kind to one another, much kinder than usual. There is a great dearth of kindness in the world today. We must redress the balance."

That evening, as well as the time I spent at the home of the Phipps' and with Maurice Baring, reawakened in my mind the image of England at her best. But the difficulty of the situation was often brought home to me in painful fashion. Relations between the two countries were becoming more acrimonious. General de Gaulle, the great expert on tanks, had recruited a legion in London, and his plans created a distressing question of conscience for many Frenchmen. Some believed the thing to do, first of all, in the hour of our country's agony, was *to maintain the unity of France*; others refused to recognize the Armistice and joined General de Gaulle.

There were recriminations by radio between London and Bordeaux, and I deplored the useless bitterness of these talks. I preached moderation, but without much success. England now was thinking only of organizing her own defenses. In May she had lacked divisions well enough equipped to be sent to France; but in July she had more than a million soldiers adequately trained to defend her territory against an invading army. Canadians and Australians were going to fight for the first time in England. Everywhere along the roads and in the cities you saw fortified positions being constructed. Profiting by our cruel experience, the high command ordered the civil population to stay at home in case of attack, and announced that the roads would be kept clear by machine guns. In each village a corps of volunteers was recruited as a defense against parachutists. Everywhere I found a spirit of resolution and desperate courage, which was new. England had received a terrible shock in the sudden discovery that the French Army was not invincible and that she was no longer secure on her island. But as always in history she was not discouraged but strengthened by danger.

On July 2nd the French Military Mission demobilized me and since, for one thing, communications no longer existed between Great Britain and France and, for another, I had agreed to deliver the "Lowell Lectures" at the Lowell Institute in Boston a little later, I decided to leave for America.

The boat on which I crossed was one of those in which England was sending children to Canada. The scene on deck was touching and amazing. A thousand children were at play in the sun around the guns that protected them. The Cruiser *Revenge* and two destroyers escorted us. It was on this boat that I learned, from a bulletin struck up in the 'tweendecks, the frightful news of the Battle of Oran.

Of all the misfortunes that had pursued us for weeks this seemed the most terrible. A Frenchman first of all, but for twenty years a friend of England, I was like a child of divorced parents who stays with his mother but who suffers nevertheless. My heart said: "My country, right or wrong." My reason deplored this break between two peoples who have so much need of each other. Leaning against the rail, I looked for a long while at the sea marbled with foam and the great cruiser gliding silently at our side. My English shipmates, respecting my sorrow, passed close beside me without speaking. Suddenly I remembered what Desmond MacCarthy had said to me one evening: "Whatever happens, let us not forget that our friends have not changed," and I began unconsciously to murmur the old Scotch song: "Should auld acquaintance be forgot . . ." High up in a turret on the *Revenge* a light went on: luminous dots and dashes were communicating a mysterious message to us.

VI

WHAT HAPPENED TO FRANCE

W HENEVER I think of that ship, loaded
with children, that took me to Canada I
feel as if I were recalling a dream. This giant,
floating nursery seemed unreal. On deck hundreds
of little folk with blond and brown curly heads
rushed about, laughed, shouted, climbed on the
rigging, hoisted themselves up the companion
stairs, fell, wept, and then laughed again. The
smallest were harnessed like ponies so that one
mother could tie to her chair, or hold, the reins of
a four-in-hand. In the same cabin with me lived
Adrian, a little boy of eight, who was making the
long voyage alone.

Throughout the whole trip Adrian proved himself a reserved and dignified companion. Educated

[158]

in an English school, trained to self-control from infancy, he was neither timid nor overbold. He tried to do everything for himself, learned to climb alone up to his berth which was above mine and very high, took a cold shower every evening, every morning folded his pajamas and put them under his pillow. He was neat, thoughtful and brave. His parents lived in Siam. When his uncle had said goodby to him in Glasgow he had given him seven shillings sixpence. That was his fortune. My own was not much larger but I was more frugal. Adrian purchased pencils, whistles and candy at the ship's store. When he arrived in Canada he had only five shillings left. His great sorrow was that he had left his bicycle in Scotland, but he had brought its headlight with him, and from time to time, when he woke up at night, he would proudly illuminate the cabin.

Sometimes I would get up at dawn and stretch out on deck in order to enjoy for a time the silent beauty of the ocean before the children took possession. At that early hour the dark and powerful *Revenge* was already conversing with us in its language of light. The destroyers played around her like puppies around their mother and sometimes one of them would dash off to a great distance in pursuit of a phantom submarine.

It was on one of these mornings that N . . . A . . . , an English writer whose books I admire and who was on his way to the United States to make a lecture tour, came and sat down near me.

"I knew you were aboard," he said, "and I take the liberty of speaking to you because there are many things I do not understand in the terrible drama of France. I am not speaking of the military defeat, which can be explained by your two countries' lack of preparation and by a wrong conception of strategy. It is the moral disaster that surprises me, and I should like to ask you some questions about it, if the subject is not too painful to you."

"Ask your questions," I said. "The subject *is* painful, but I do not try to run away from my own thoughts."

He stretched himself out on the deckchair beside mine.

"Does it seem to you true to say," he asked, "that the spirit of the French Army and the French people was not as good in 1939 as in 1914 and that the will to win was less strong?"

"Many units of the army fought splendidly, but it is true that the war spirit in the French people as a whole was less fiery than in 1914."

"And why? The fate of France was at stake in both instances and the menace greater in 1940."

"That's true, but the France of 1914 was a relatively united country; the France of 1940 was a profoundly disunited country."

"Hasn't France been a divided nation ever since 1793?"

"Chateaubriand said of the Terror that this bloody ditch would never be filled in. And it is certain that memories of the Revolution dominated the political life of France for a long time. But in 1914 there was a sincere reconciliation in the face of the enemy. It was the time of the 'Union Sacrée.' For four years socialists and capitalists, radicals and monarchists, were brothers in arms. Peace wrote an end to that idyll. The Russian Revolution inspired new hopes in the laboring class and new fears in the middle class. Part of the latter naïvely thought, first that Fascism, and then that Nazism,

[161]

would be a rampart against Communism. The authoritarian governments at Moscow and Berlin acted in opposition to each other while biding their time to form an alliance. Both expended huge sums for propaganda and exerted themselves to seduce the French masses. These alien hands tore anew a deep fissure between the two halves of France."

"When did the 'Union Sacrée' cease to exist?"

"Almost immediately after the war. In 1934 the street fighting of the sixth of February showed the gravity of the situation. It manifested itself again in 1936 when the seizure of the factories, workshops and stores alienated from the government a large number of the lower middle class who until then had supported it. With the exception of a small minority of unfair employers, everybody in France agreed on the necessity of social reforms, but the methods forced on the Blum government by the Communists were violent and clumsy. France is a country of enclosures, of walls, of fences, of shutters and of closed ledgers; the invasion by a force of private property awakened unpleasant emotions. Side by side with a Fifth Column, made up of actual traitors who were *not at all* numerous, there grew up a whole army of malcontents who, without knowing it, contributed their unconscious support to foreign propaganda. On the day when Russia became Germany's ally the Communists at once swelled the battalions of this Grand Army of defection. Add to this the fact that the causes of this war were not well understood by the combatants. In 1914 France had been invaded; the situation was clear. In 1939 France herself had declared war on account of Dantzig, a city of which many Frenchmen did not know the location or even the existence. Those who were better informed understood that this was only a surface appearance and that if we permitted our allies to be gobbled up, one after the other, we should end by being gobbled up ourselves. But the others argued that it was England who had dragged us into this adventure and that the war might have been avoided."

"I imagine England has been unpopular in France for a long time?"

"It's not as simple as that. The curve of English unpopularity in our country has had abrupt variations. England was extremely unpopular at the time of the Sanctions. Many Frenchmen, particularly in the army, favored courting the friendship of Italy. The latter gave them very little encouragement, but after a long period of Franco-Italian quarrels the Accord of Stresa allowed them the hope that henceforth England, Italy and France would maintain the peace of Europe. To sacrifice the support of the Italian Army and Air Force in order to preserve the independence of the Negus seemed insane to many Frenchmen. Even those who did not approve the violence of certain newspaper articles hostile to England and who continued to feel esteem for her, believed her foreign policy was imprudent and disastrous.

"A little later, at the time of the general election of 1936, conservative England seemed to be supporting the Popular Front and this puzzled and irritated a considerable section of the French middle class. On the other hand, in 1937, the visit of the British sovereigns to Paris and, in 1938, Neville Chamberlain's desire for peace, touched this same section of public opinion. . . . In everything I am saying here I am neither criticizing nor approving; I am simply describing."

"You speak of the middle class, but weren't the

sentiments of the working class quite different?
There, I imagine, Eden was popular and Chamberlain disliked?"

"That's not entirely so. In the Socialist party it self the appeasement movement, which had the support of Paul Faure and his friends, was very powerful. When the newspaper *Paris-Soir* started a subscription to present a house in France to Mr. Chamberlain, it was the poorer readers who subscribed. You must not forget that France is a country of small tradesmen, of peasant owners, and not a country of proletarians. In the army it is the middle class, together with the country nobility, the school teachers and the priests, that supply the reserve officers. It is impossible for a French government to carry on war successfully without the support of the factory workers, but no less impossible unless the middle class is with it, and wholeheartedly with it."

"And in this war the middle class did not cooperate?"

"It cooperated because of military discipline and because of its old tradition of patriotism, but with no enthusiasm. For more than twenty years the newspapers they read had been saying the worst things they could think of about the government, the politicians, the ministers, about all those, in short, who were to be their leaders in war. It was a dangerous preparation. Faith is needed in order to fight. Of course this lack of support was not the essential cause of the disaster. If our armies had had the necessary equipment, the guns, airplanes and tanks, and if they had scored an initial victory, the state of mind of the middle class would have been transformed. France is an old military nation. It has Valmy and Austerlitz in its blood. Enthusiasm would have mounted in the hearts of the most rebellious, ready to spring forth. But retreat and defeat had the contrary effect of liberating all the grievances and rancors. 'After all,' thought many officers and soldiers, 'after all, our political leaders are paying for their mistakes!' And to their sincere and terrible despair at seeing their country vanquished, was added the barely perceptible thought that justice had been satisfied."

"You say: 'If our armies had had the necessary equipment,' and in your eyes this lack of airplanes and tanks is the principal cause of your misfortunes. But let's push the analysis further: Why were you lacking in equipment?"

"In the first place because the General Staff, holding a mistaken military theory, did not order in time the airplanes, tanks and the anti-tank and antiaircraft guns which were indispensable. And then because, for several years, the workmen in our factories had done little work and done it badly. Finally because certain manufacturers, more interested in their own profits than in the safety of France, had carried on a campaign to prevent the purchase abroad of equipment which, however, they were unable to supply themselves. Before the war, when the government was ready to order airplanes from the United States, the Parliamentary Commissions, influenced by these underhand campaigns, only authorized the purchase of one hundred, a ridiculous number."

"But why did the government show such weakness in dealing both with the businessmen and the workmen? When one's country is in danger private interests and desires should be quiet. It is the duty of the government to impose silence upon them. Why did the government fail to govern? Even the

[167]

most ignorant saw the approach of war and the growing strength of Germany. Was the form of government at fault? But in 1914 the form of government was the same and yet . . ."

"In 1914 there was no enemy propaganda; in 1939 it had been at work for five or six years with diabolical adroitness. Now democracies are a form of government in which public opinion is all-powerful and in which nothing can be done without its support. Examine the facts in France, in England and in the United States; you will find that public opinion in these three countries has been mistaken, or has been misled, with surprising consistency. It has not realized the danger and demanded rearmament until *much* too late."

"Their leaders could and should have directed public opinion."

"Unfortunately political leaders have grown accustomed to consulting opinion rather than guiding it. You see them leaning on public opinion, sounding it out and trying to find some way in which they can, at once, please it and convince it respectfully that it is better for a country to live

[168]

than to die. As for the military leaders, they were dependent upon the political leaders and they dared neither oppose nor importune them. For lack of strict, precise orders, the departments and the experts took their time. No one in our country made out a timetable of operations. In Germany Hitler said: 'I wish to be in Paris on the 15th of June. To do that I must open the offensive at the beginning of May. To open the offensive at the beginning of May I need new tanks at the beginning of April.' Thus he drew his blueprints and woe to him who did not carry them out! What happened in our case? The experts were asked: 'How much time do you need to build so many airplanes a month, or so many tanks?' The experts picked a date at random and their decision was respected. We made our timetables backward. It was the war that should have governed technical exigencies, not the technicians who should have controlled military requirements. As a result we made preparations for a war in 1942 which was over in 1940."

"In short you, or rather we, forgot that *time* is one of the most important factors in any action."

"Say *the* most important. Hitler's greatest

strength was to do things quickly and to act while we were deliberating."

"And do you attribute this sluggishness to the parliamentary form of government?"

"I believe that a courageous leader, more interested in national safety than in his own political career, could have forced Parliament and even the recalcitrant departments to act with the necessary speed. Churchill seems to have succeeded in doing it in England. The decree granting to the British government powers as great as any dictator has ever possessed was voted in a few minutes. But it is a fact that the parliamentary form of government, invented by England, functions a little less badly there than in any other country."

"And why did this form of government fail to function well in France?"

"For many reasons. In the first place the French and British governments had hardly anything in common except the word Parliament; in reality they were entirely different. When Professor Barker of Cambridge delivered his remarkable lecture at the Sorbonne in Paris on the political government of England, he began with this sentence:

TRAGEDY IN FRANCE

'*England is a democracy because she is an aristocracy.*' That paradox was true. In England Parliament was the house of country gentlemen before it became that of the whole nation. In the course of centuries it grew, in their eyes, to be a kind of club, one of the most exclusive, with strange and ancient customs of its own, and the defender of liberties. It is a tradition in many noble English families to send a younger son to the House of Commons. There the descendants of the ancient aristocracy meet the representatives of the new leadership which a great country produces in each generation. Winston Churchill belongs to the Marlborough family, but he filled out his Cabinet with workmen's sons, like Ernest Bevin, who are his most efficient ministers. Thus in England the people's government had the benefit of historical experience. In France, for a long time, the divorce between Parliament and the real leaders of the country in culture, business and labor had been very nearly complete. Most of the professional politicians were lawyers who knew how to review a case but did not know how to act and did not seem able to separate their personal practice from the business of the state. At the time of the Stavisky case their attitude shocked and exasperated a large part of the nation which ceased to believe in the democratic régime. Both the extreme Right and the extreme Left had recourse to methods of violence. This meant the end of parliamentary government."

"One thing is sure," he said, "the day the struggle between parties becomes a struggle between classes, parliamentary government can no longer function. What, as a matter of fact, is necessary for this form of government? That one party shall assume power, in place of another, when such is the freely expressed desire of the majority and that the minority shall acquiesce freely and without violence in being governed, for a stated period, by the majority. What is the necessary and sufficient condition for this acquiescence on the part of the minority? *It is the assurance that the majority will act fairly.* In a parliamentary and democratic form of government it must never happen that the assumption of power by one party shall be considered as the beginning of persecution by the remainder of the country. In England the Liberals and Conservatives could accept without trepidation the alternation of parties, and this is still true today of the Conservatives and the Labor Party because the Labor Party, while defending the interests of the British workmen, has refused to become a revolutionary party."

"In France," I said, "the working of the parliamentary machine was wholly thrown out of gear on the day when the Socialist Party, which had become the largest in Parliament, allied itself with the Communists. You can choose between a totalitarian philosophy and a parliamentary system, but you certainly cannot have both. You could not expect the French middle class to accept as a normal event in government the assumption of power by men whose avowed program was the destruction of that very class. From the moment when fear and passion *in both camps* became greater than the love of country, French democracy was a house divided against itself and no longer capable of winning a military victory."

N—— A—— lit a cigarette and smoked for some time in silence, watching the sea gulls that accompanied us resting nonchalantly on the waves.

"If we go to the bottom of the problem," he said, "the real struggle going on at this moment is not between two forms of government—democracy and dictatorship—but between two philosophies. In the Eighteenth Century, as a result of the brilliant advances in science, men believed that reason was all-powerful and that it was possible to reconstruct society through the use of the intelligence. That was too optimistic a view of human nature. The theories of Rousseau, despite the fact that he was a 'man of good will,' gave rise to the Terror, which led twenty years later to the restoration of the King of France and a White Terror. Throughout the Nineteenth Century the liberal experiment went on, with occasional returns to Authoritarianism, such as the Second Empire in France. In those countries where this experiment failed (Italy, Russia, Germany, Spain) a wholly contrary doctrine, brutal and pessimistic, was launched against the optimism of the Eighteenth Century. Faith in reason had been the characteristic of the Eighteenth Century; the men of the Twentieth Century—Lenin, Mussolini and Hitler—sang the praises of violence. The Eighteenth Century had believed in truth and in the possibility of discovering it by the methods of science; the men of the Twentieth Century know no other truth than the one they choose according to their needs and impose through their propaganda."

"There is," I said, "an astonishing text, very well written by the way; it is the preface composed by Mussolini for Machiavelli's *Prince*. Its theme is the complete pessimism of which you speak: man, according to Il Duce, is a wholly depraved animal; he is not to be understood except by one who begins by despising him; all means are legitimate in governing because, if there is not a tyrant, a country falls into anarchy which, says Mussolini, is worse than tyranny."

"Today," he replied, "those who despise man are in the ascendant. Will it be a permanent triumph? I don't think so. Nothing is permanent in human affairs. Thesis, antithesis, synthesis, Hegel was right about it. *Thesis of the Eighteenth Century:* man is born good; the voice of the people is the voice of God. *Antithesis of the Twentieth Century:* man is a despicable monster who must be controlled by force; the people must listen to the voice of their master. The synthesis will come: Christianity has already made it. The doctrine of original sin and redemption was a moral synthesis. And what will our political synthesis be? Approximately this: man was originally a cruel animal that has been gradually civilized by human and divine laws; he gained his liberties through work and discipline; he can only preserve them through work and discipline; democracies in order to survive must remember the virtues by which they came into being."

"The word republic," I said, "seems to me finer than the word democracy because it contains that idea of devotion to the public interest, to the *res publica*, which I consider essential. England, though a monarchy, is a republic by virtue of that devotion, which is taught in all her schools. The French Republic quickly restored itself after 1870 and was even able to conquer an empire because the Republic was then an ideal for which the first Republicans were ready to make sacrifices. It perished on the day when its statesmen put their personal interests and personal feelings before the public good. . . . I knew Poincaré well; I admit that he was a narrow-minded man. 'Why do you want to go to London?' he once asked me. 'As soon as one leaves the Place de la Concorde, one ceases to make sense.' But he *had* the republican virtues. His honesty was so exacting that he never allowed a doorman at the ministry, who was paid by the state, to do him a personal service. After forty years of public life, and of almost uninterrupted power, he was a poor man. . . . Examine the private lives of the great English statesmen: they were unblemished. Gladstone hated Disraeli, and Disraeli had no love for Peel, but all three were good husbands and honest men. That's what makes good nations. Montesquieu has said, unless I am mistaken, that honor is the mainspring of monarchies, virtue that of republics."

There was a long silence, then he said:

"In short what are the essential liberties that we want to safeguard at all costs? We want the law to be the same for all, thus assuring equality of opportunities; we want each man to have free access to the sources of information (and this is the true meaning of liberty of thought) ; we want each man to be free to express his ideas so long as he does not advocate the destruction of the state which gives him this freedom; and we want the government to be changed when that is the freely expressed will of the majority. It seems to me that's all. . . ."

"That's all," I said, "and it does not mean that each day, before taking action, statesmen must sound out public opinion and consult it as though it were an oracle. A country can be perfectly free even if the leaders she has chosen do not consult her on each particular move. If in 1936 the English Ministers had had the wisdom to disregard public opinion and support France, we should have avoided this war."

The sun had risen higher in the sky. The curly headed small folk were beginning to invade the deck. Balls were rolling among the deck chairs.

"Those balls!" he said. "If we had only left them to children perhaps we should have paid more heed to the dangers that were threatening us. It is a fact that for a long time our countries, rather than face a painful reality which demanded work and courage, took refuge in make-believe worlds. England lived for cricket and football; the United States for baseball and the movies; France for local politics and literary cliques. Sport and art are excellent means of escape when the needs of security have been met; but to put them ahead of all other activities at a time when vital problems have not been

solved is the height of collective folly. Politics itself became a sport. But when it is a question of
saving your skin time is too precious to permit of
these mass escapes. While our children were being
delightfully thrilled by the happy endings of
Hollywood movies the youth of Germany was at
work shaping the real world. . . . And in it the
endings are harsh."

He got up.

"It's breakfast time," he said. "Porridge and eggs
and bacon are realities that I for one don't despise."

Left alone I spent a long time thinking about this
conversation. I took out a pencil and, on the jacket
of the book I was reading, which was a novel by
Balzac, I wrote this:

"REMEDIES: *To be strong.* A nation that is
not ready to die for its liberties will lose
them.

To act quickly. Ten thousand airplanes built
in time are better than fifty thousand after
the battle.

To direct opinion. A leader shows the way;
he does not follow.

To preserve a united country. Political par-

ties are passengers aboard the same ship; if
they wreck it, all will perish.

*To protect public opinion against the influ-
ences of foreign governments.* To defend
ideas is legitimate; to accept money from
abroad for defending them is a crime.

*To punish immediately and severely any il-
legal violence.* Incitement to illegal violence
is a crime.

*To protect youth against teaching calculated
to weaken the unity of the country.* A state
that does not try to preserve itself commits
suicide.

*To demand that those who govern lead up-
right lives.* Vice of any kind gives a foothold
to the enemy.

*To believe passionately in the ideas and in
the way of life for which you are fighting.*
It is faith that creates armies and even arms.
Liberty deserves to be served with more passion than tyranny."

That is as far as I had gone when Adrian ran up
holding out to me a bleeding finger.

[180]

"I have cut myself," he said. "Do you know anything about bandaging?"

I did the best I could.

I arrived in Halifax on the twelfth of July and next day went by train to Montreal. On the station platform, amid the reporters who greeted me in French with that slight accent, Norman and archaic, which gives so much charm to the conversation of French Canadians, I found my wife again, whom I had left on the tenth of June in Paris and from whom I had had no news during all the time I was in England. She told me her adventures.

Leaving Neuilly-sur-Seine (where we lived) at dawn on the eleventh of June, she had found herself in that uninterrupted line of cars on the road from Paris to Orléans which moved forward at the rate of a man walking. Near Dourdan German airplanes, in three successive waves, flew over the refugees and machine-gunned them. The guards forced my wife and her travelling companions to lie down in the ditches. Near her, children were wounded in the shoulder and thigh, but no one was killed.

She spent the night in her car at Vierzon among

thousands of families who had no other home except their automobiles and next day reached our country home in Parigord. More than a hundred refugees were already installed there. From there she tried to get in touch with me in London but all her telegrams remained unanswered. After five days she became alarmed and left for Bordeaux where she found a heart-rending spectacle—the end of a society.

The administrative framework of France, which had seemed so solid to us, had fallen to pieces under the bombs of the German Air Force. *Because it did not have the mastery of the air, the government had lost the mastery of the earth*. The police had given up all attempt to maintain order. At Bordeaux you could go into the office of the Premier or the President of the Republic without being stopped or announced. Ambassadors were wandering about in the local college where an office had been set up to tell them which chateaux in the vicinity had been assigned to them. The ambassadors' wives, covered with sweat and draped with pearls, were being cooked by slow degrees in their Rolls Royces on the Allées de Tourny. My wife, encountering one of our friends, who was a cabinet minister, learned that Paul Reynaud was going to resign and that the new government would ask for an armistice.

"I thought," she said, "the war was going to be continued from North Africa?"

"That," he replied, "was Reynaud's program, but it was defeated in the Council of Ministers by a vote of thirteen to ten . . . Reynaud must be closeted with President Lebrun now . . . I believe he hopes that an armistice cannot be arranged and that he will be recalled, but that's a dream. The armistice will be signed and the Germans will be here within a week . . . You would do well to leave."

"Where shall I go?" my wife said. "If the armistice is signed, my husband will be demobilized in London. Will he be able to get back to France?"

"That's unlikely. Communications between France and England have almost ceased to exist."

My wife knew that I had promised to deliver the Lowell Lectures; she decided to go to the United States and wait for me there. As she had with her letters from the Lowell Institute she had no trouble in obtaining visas. She was happy to leave Bordeaux where she had been sickened by the egoism and indifference of the many people who sipped ancient and noble vintages in the "rococo" grottoes of the *Chapon Fin* while France was in agony.

On the evening of June seventeenth when she was crossing the international bridge from Hendaye to Irun my wife encountered French *douaniers* who were weeping.

"But why, Madame," they said, "have we been beaten? After all, couldn't we have continued this war? Aren't they going to leave us at least a little France? Is it true that they're going to come as far as this?"

After the scenes she had just witnessed at Bordeaux, the patriotism of these humble folk warmed her heart.

Finally at Lisbon on the fifteenth of June, thanks to faithful friends who had made the trip with her, she was able to take passage on the Yankee Clipper. As soon as she arrived in New York she sent me a cable in care of the French Embassy in London. I replied at once telling her of my coming, but the British censorship did not allow me to indicate the date of departure or the name of the boat.

Finally she learned from the American newspapers that I was on my way to Canada. It was thus that she was able to come to meet me, at six in the morning, on the platform of the Windsor Station in Montreal.

Our happiness at being reunited was mixed with the dreadful sadness of talking about the misfortunes of France.

"Do you know," my wife said, "that today is the Fourteenth of July? And do you remember? Last year in Paris . . . That splendid revue in the Champs Élysées . . . How happy and proud everyone was!"

It was indeed the Fourteenth of July. At some of the windows in Montreal fluttered the flags of France. The French Canadians were loyal.

"May France in her turn," I thought, "be loyal to herself. . . ."

II

Notes and Observations

Translated by F. L. Ludman

TEN COMMANDMENTS FOR BRITISH SOLDIERS IN FRANCE

These were written at the beginning of the War at the request of the Adjutant General and published in the Routine Orders of the British Army.

I. Remember that in the eyes of the French who see you, you represent England. It is on your uniform, your conduct and your discipline that they will judge our country.

II. Remember that the farm which is only a temporary cantonment for your battalion is home for some French soldier, whose memories bind him to every object it contains. Ask yourself: "If the war were being waged on our soil and the French were occupying *my* home, how should I wish them to behave?"

[189]

III. If you have come to France for the first time, be careful not to judge the French too hastily. Their customs are different from yours: it is no reason to think them inferior. Remember the last war and the part the French Army played in it. With means which appeared small enough to us, France achieved results which were anything but small.

IV. Tell yourself that attitudes of mind which seem natural to you because they are what you are accustomed to in Great Britain, can, without your realising it, shock and even wound a Frenchman. Britishers like human beings to treat one another with a certain amount of indifference. Your allies demand more than that. Always show a French friend a little more consideration than you would an English friend.

V. The women of the houses in which you are living will often be under your sole protection. Treat them as you would like your own wives and daughters to be treated in your absence. You will see them in the French country districts engaged in very heavy work and doing their best to replace their men. As far as your military duties allow you, help them.

VI. Strive to become good soldiers. Our enemy is trying by this long respite and these false alarms to lull us to sleep and weary us. Make good use of all this waiting and make exercises of the false alarms. Make yourselves familiar with your arms. Apply yourself to making your battalion, your battery or your squadron a crack unit. What time and tradition have done for famous regiments you now have the opportunity and leisure to do for yours. Attach great importance to the details of your clothing and your discipline. The value of an army lies in its habits.

VII. France is entrusting to your guardianship a sector of her frontier, which has become our own. It is a great honour. Never yield an inch of French ground.

VIII. Take care never to spread or listen to rumours. The object of enemy propaganda is to sow unrest and panic. Only repeat what you are certain of. Whoever says: "I haven't seen it myself, but I've heard about it," may become, without realising it, an agent of the enemy. Be an example of coolness. Yours is supposed to be a phlegmatic race. It is a fine reputation. Deserve it.

IX. Study the French language while you are in

France. Help your hosts to learn English. The task of our two countries is not only to win the war, but to win the peace afterwards. This they will only be able to do if they remain united: they will only remain united if they understand one another.

X. The alliance of France and England has been a political and military necessity: it must become a human reality. These two countries, which need one another, must hold one another in unreserved esteem. It is up to YOU to see that the Englishman is regarded as an ally worthy of trust and affection by ten, twenty—a hundred Frenchmen.

TEN COMMANDMENTS FOR THE CIVILIAN IN TIME OF WAR

These were written between the Battle of Flanders and the Battle of the Somme.

I. Whatever risks you are running, whatever restrictions you are subjected to, whatever difficulties you encounter, think of the lot of the fighting men at this moment and say to yourself: "I am too well off."

II. Do your best at your job. In peace-time you did what you could. Nothing more was asked of you. In war-time you must do infinitely more than you can.

III. Never repeat a piece of news you have not verified or had from a source that is French and trustworthy. Every pessimistic rumour forges an arm for the enemy.

IV. Never repeat a piece of news which, even if true, is still secret. The desire to appear well-informed is so keen in some of us that it overrides our prudence, our patriotism, even our care for our own safety.

V. Never buy up uselessly things that are necessary to the soldiers. Do not travel unless you must. Tomorrow a tank or an airplane that is protecting you may have to go short of the petrol you have wasted.

VI. Wait until there is real danger before you get worried. If an airplane drops bombs on the countryside, you have little more chance of being touched than of winning the big prize in the national lottery.

VII. Whatever happens, keep calm. If you feel nervous, ask your doctor to help you. We are not always masters of our bodies, but we can school our bodies to obey our wills.

VIII. Do not allow your mood to be swayed by the rise and fall of the battle. Before you rejoice or lament wait for a victory or a reverse. In the arsenal of France your nerves play a part. Use them carefully.

IX. Seek security in things eternal: faith, patriotism, wisdom. Only great feelings and great books are worthy of great moments.

X. Believe in France. She has known a hundred invasions. She has survived them. She will live.

KING GEORGE VISITS HIS ARMIES

This and the two following pieces were written in November and December, 1939.

I

"THE KING is coming to France. . . ." It was first of all a mystery, then a secret, then a rumor. Those who knew did not talk: those who talked did not know. All the same, the visit had to be prepared for. It was then announced at G.H.Q. that "an illustrious personage" would be coming. The war correspondents used a code when they had to discuss the taboo in front of strangers. They spoke of when "Mrs. Harris" would be coming—when she would be at Arras. A notice put up in the room that was reserved for them read: "During Mrs. Harris' visit, the telephone will be open until eleven o'clock." Prudence justified the liberty.

Finally the troops themselves were told. To see their joy was a joy in itself. Their loyalty had nothing artificial about it. To these men, living on a foreign soil, far from their native cities, their homes and their families, the King's visit would bring something of England. The face that they all knew, remembered particularly by some at the Coronation, by others in a scouts' camp, by others in the slums of some great city, would bring back to all of them the pictures that hang on the walls of every farm and cottage, and awaken the poetry of the old country they love so well.

It is a feeling that has nothing in common with the mixture of terror and devotion with which their strange master inspires our enemies. This young man, so unassuming, so pleasant and yet so dignified, personifies a long lineage and a noble history. Twenty-five years ago, his father before him visited the fathers of the men who are welcoming him today. The affection which binds the British soldier to his sovereign is, in all its aspects, the affection of a family—a family which has grown into an Empire.

That is why the Royal Visit is an important event. It quickens pulses and reawakens energies. For a week the whole army had been giving a more especial attention to its uniform, its arms, its drill. The few careless ones who, in the face of strict orders, sometimes forgot their gas-masks, saw and remembered the King's example of obedience. As for the French villagers, they listened to the cheering of the soldiers, saw the steel helmets and forage-caps in the air, looked on in wonder at the massive march-past and nodded their heads and muttered:

"Ah, yes. . . . It's a great country all right."

II

It would have been hard to imagine a more pleasing setting for the review. In the background, an eighteenth-century French chateau, long and low, broken by isolated clumps of fine old trees. Identical sheep grazed quietly up a grassy slope. The whole décor had the noble and wise negligence of the great English parklands. A touch of gold was added by the group of French and English Generals at the gates. The bands of the Guards, drum and fife, stood massed before the chateau.

A car bearing the tricolor arrived with General

Giraud in his long, light coat. The sound of *"V'la Castellane qui passe"* sped across the fields and its notes from the fifes, fell strangely on our ears. The motorcyclists . . . the escort . . . the King. . . . The drummers raised their sticks, perfectly horizontal, to the level of their mouths and it was a *God Save the King* different from all others, that ended magnificently in a fervent cry from the fifes and a long roll of the drums.

And the March Past. . . . The King stood in the gateway with the French Generals around him. Twenty yards before the saluting-point the officers gave "Eyes Left," twenty yards beyond it, "Eyes Front." The heads turned abruptly as if mounted on a single pivot. They were all giants, these men. Battalion followed battalion. One command alternated with the other. The King saluted each platoon all during its march past and never relaxed for one moment except between the companies. He looked young, vigorous, happy.

After lunch, the troops paraded on the lawns of the chateau. So long were the khaki lines that their ends were lost in the mist that hung above the hedgerows. The King passed slowly between the

ranks and that evening the men would be writing
proudly to their womenfolk: "It was great . . . I
was so close to the King I could have touched him."
The review ended, the Brigadier, his steel helmet
in his hand, opened the gates that had been holding in check that mighty flood of enthusiasm:

"Three cheers for His Majesty the King!"

The British cheers rolled away across the French
fields and they in their turn echoed a muffled
"Hurrah . . . Hurrah!"

The sheep browsed on, imperturbable.

III

When the King moves through one long day
from a battery to an air-field, from an infantry
brigade to a tank section, it is naturally impossible
for all the war correspondents to follow him from
place to place. But everything must be reported
and so the correspondents adopt the method of
pooling their information. All observations are
made available to everybody. Each man uses the
details he thinks most important or picturesque.
What he chooses, and of course his style, give the
article its individuality.

"The King," the chairman began, "travelled eighty miles today. He left his residence at 8:15 and saw the airmen first. Sir Philip Gibbs, who was there, will give you an account of the visit."

"There was a strong and very cold wind," said Sir Philip. "When the King arrived, the men who had flown over Germany were presented to him and he asked them for a few details of the flight. He then saw the young Flight Commander who brought down a German bomber the other day."

"What did the King say to him?"

"The King said, 'Go and do it again.'"

"You cannot publish that," cut in the censor.

"Why?"

"There is no 'why' . . . you are not allowed to . . . that's all."

"Very well. . . . The King asked how the patrol worked. It was suggested that he himself should give the take-off signal, which he did. In thirty seconds, the men were in the air. Before leaving the air-field, as it was getting colder and colder, the King drank a cup of tea."

"China or Indian?" asked some purist.

"China."

"Then," the chairman said, "the King visited the Nth Division. Mr. W——, who was there, will tell you the story."

W—— got up and, among other things, told how the King had stopped in front of a soldier and said:

"Didn't I decorate you the other day in London for an act of bravery?"

This was found to be correct and called forth long commentaries on the prodigious memory of the Royal Family.

The account continued . . . machine-guns . . . artillery . . . the speech of welcome made by the Mayor of a French village . . . pill-boxes the King inspected . . . lunch. . . .

"Before the King arrived, we went into the inn where His Majesty was to lunch. It was kept by a rather pretty woman of about thirty-five whose sick child was being attended by an English army doctor. When she learned she was going to receive the King, she went into the nearest town for flowers, which she presented to him very gracefully."

"What sort of flowers?"

"Red carnations."

"What was the menu?"

"Chicken pie, Christmas pudding, cheese. . . . The sergeant who acted as headwaiter told me afterwards that the King refused the pudding. . . . After the escort had left, we asked 'Madame' for her impressions of the King. . . . She said he was very nice and 'unassuming.' . . ."

"Who was at the lunch?"

"We are only allowed to mention the Duke of Gloucester, the Commander in Chief, and the Corps Commanders."

Now and again, when one of the narrators waxed sentimental or stilted, the audience, which was possessed of a very lively sense of humor, applauded ironically. But it was rather to conceal their own feelings. They were very proud of their young King who had just acquitted himself of a difficult task with, to use Madame's expression, such "unassuming" perfection.

RECONNAISSANCE SQUADRON

"DOC! The wireless. . . . We must have the six o'clock news. . . ."

The doctor, who wore the blue-gray uniform of the Royal Air Force, rose from a weighty volume on anaesthetics and switched it on.

". . . Norwegian troops are entrenched near Elverum, about eighty miles north of Oslo and are resisting German attacks. . . ."

The ten young heads round the table were raised. The squadron's leader was no more than twenty-five years old. To his officers he was, affectionately, "Ginger," but his face, under the bright hair, had a marked strength and his authority was unquestioned. Near him a few officers were either writing letters of their own, or censoring their men's. Outside, the rain and hail beat steadily on the window-panes.

"In Stavanger harbour a German warship has been sunk by a Norwegian vessel."

The bell of the field telephone quivered, became insistent. The officer nearest lifted the receiver.

"Number N. squadron. . . . Ginger, it's for you. . . . *Wing*. . . . They probably want us to go and inspect the midnight sun."

The squadron leader rose and took the receiver. As he listened he raised his eyebrows a little.

"Very good. . . . Yes. . . . Yes, sir. . . . We'll do that. . . ."

Then, as he hung up:

"Headquarters want," he said, "three reconnaissances over Germany: one tonight, another at dawn tomorrow, and the other about nine o'clock. . . . Whose turn to go?"

"Watson," somebody said, "Grant, and Turner for night pilot."

"They're to be at *Wing* at eight to get their orders."

The wireless had been turned off. Now there was no sound but the drumming of the hail on the windows. Over the table a heavy silence had fallen. It was not that a reconnaissance flight over Germany was a rare exploit for these youngsters—

theirs was a squadron that had photographed the whole Siegfried Line and scores of German hide-outs. But the weather . . .

"It's a *flop*," said Watson sadly. Watson was one of the pilots who was to go.

I understood from this remark that this was a time when things were not all they should be, just as I knew that "gen" referred to a pilot's general knowledge ("He has a good 'gen.' "), "met." the meteorological report, and "reco." reconnaissance.

"What was the half-past four met. like?"

"Clouds at two thousand, turning to rain from three thousand; ice formation at three thousand."

"Humph!"

ORDERS

An hour later I went with Watson to *Wing* Headquarters accompanied by his navigator, a sergeant, and his gunner, a mechanic with laughing eyes. We made our way to the Intelligence Office. On one of its walls hung a large map of Germany studded with red, blue and gold, to indicate anti-aircraft gun-sites, balloon barrages and squadrons.

"What G.H.Q. wants to know," said the Wing

Commander, "is whether there are any troop movements of importance in this region." He stood on
a chair and indicated a German province. "And
in this. . . . And if so, in what direction the
movements are taking place. . . . Here's your
itinerary."

The sergeant-navigator, serious and painstaking,
wrote in the log the details of the route, the reconnaissance signals, the zones to be observed. The
gunner, less concerned, rocked his shoulders and
looked at the maps and photographs around him.
Below, in the *Wing* mess-room, Turner, the night
pilot, was playing darts while he waited to take off.

"Two tens. . . . You're beaten, Padre. . . .
What says the met.?"

"No change."

"Right!"

But he looked worried.

THE RETURN

At dawn the next day, I heard the hum of Watson's machine over the village. I ran to the window.
The weather was still appalling and the plane was
lost in clouds. I thought of the sergeant bent over

his map in the front; the gunner in the tail, watching for the enemy. Towards nine o'clock I went to Wing for news. I had hardly arrived when we were reassured by telephone.

"Watson's back. All's well. . . ."

A car left for the air-field and brought back the three men, still in flying dress and fur-lined boots.

"What? In four hours you've been able to go into Germany, observe a wide region and get back again?"

"Of course. . . . It's not very far. . . ."

"Were you attacked?"

"It seems we were. . . . But I saw nothing I'm glad to say. My observer and gunner told me afterwards. . . ."

"Was their shooting any good?"

"Not at all good I understand. . . . What amused my gunner was the sight of an enemy fighter that tried to chase us being fired on by his own guns."

One of the Wing officers came in with sherry, cheese and biscuits. While the three men ate, the staff officer heard their account of the flight, following it on the map.

"Many trains on this line?"

"No, sir—just normal traffic."

"What about this river?"

"A few chains of barges going north."

"Did you get any photographs?"

"Yes, but I shouldn't think they'd be very good."

While he answered the questions I looked at Watson. With his high, fur-topped boots and young face he might have been a boy back from school. The gunner of the laughing eyes was rocking his shoulders to and fro. While the staff officer spoke to Headquarters, the pilot turned to me.

"Dreams are extraordinary things," he said. "Last night, before we took off, I dreamed I was on reconnaissance in Germany, but in a train. . . . Yes, I was in some German station. . . . My mother was on the platform and a porter was shouting at me: 'Nach Essen!' . . . Absurd, wasn't it?"

A STROLL WITH THE PADRE

"GOOD morning, Padre."

"Good morning, Biddle. . . . Out of hospital I see."

"Yes, Padre."

A Church of England chaplain was the padre of these gunners. He was built like an athlete, with fine open features that shone happily over his black stock.

The men greeted him cheerfully.

"It took some time," he told me, "to gain their confidence. Now they come quite voluntarily to tell me their family troubles. The poor Biddle lad, who just saluted you, managed to make himself very ill indeed a fortnight ago when he got inoculated three times against typhoid."

"What? Three times!"

"Yes, three times. You see, when the whole brigade was being vaccinated against typhoid, there were three doctors working at three separate tables. . . . There was a long queue up to each of the tables. The unfortunate Biddle thought he had to go to each of the tables in turn. Hence the three injections.

"Good Lord! The reaction must have been pretty violent."

"It was terrifying. But anyway, he seems to have got over it."

The wind and the rain on the plateau were so fierce that we were nearly swept off the wooden causeway that led to the battery. And it was a great relief to stumble down the muddy steps into a hole warmed by a fireplace contrived from petrol tins. Nevertheless, the chimney drew very well. Here we found an officer and a few gunners.

"What do you do all day in this hole of yours?" I asked.

"My men write letters and I censor them."

He looked at the formidable pile that had accumulated on his table and gauged it with an expert eye.

"There's about an hour-and-a-half's censoring there," he said, "but by the time I've got 'em finished, they'll have written just such another pile. It's appalling!"

At a table of white wood the gunners sat writing with great concentration their interminable epistles.

"But what can they find to say?"

"It hardly ever varies. . . . 'I am well. The food is good. We are living in mud . . .' and the rest is family affairs, household tiffs that last a couple of weeks—which is the length of time it takes to exchange two or three letters. There's also my official correspondence. It's quite funny now and again."

"For instance?"

"Well, you know the predictor—that delicate bit of machinery that, given the elements of the problem, tells you where to fire. This machine, as you've seen, is standing there fully exposed to squalls of rain. The other day I saw that it was tarnishing a little inside and getting indistinct. I wrote to the War Office for advice and what do you think they wrote back? *'The predictor should*

*always be kept in a warm place and protected from
the damp.'*

"And what was your reply?"

"Just two words: *'Says you.'* "

"One of the most beautiful military replies I've
ever heard of," said the Padre, "was given in India
by a captain who had lost a steamroller, and who
was asked by the Government of India for an explanation. On the form he received he wrote, after
the words *'Reason for the loss,' 'Eaten by white
ants.'* He never heard another word."

One of the men came and laid a finished letter
on the captain's table. The captain sighed.

"Well, Sir," the soldier said, "are you obliged
to read it? Haven't you any confidence in your
gunners?"

"No," said the captain, "I know them too well."

He accompanied us outside.

"No airplanes to shoot at?"

"I'm afraid not. There's no hope in weather like
this. . . . And what exasperates the men is that
during the last fortnight they have had ten warnings or more and each time they have loaded the
gun the 'all clear' has been given before they could

fire it. So they've had to put the shell back again.
. . . It was always the same shell and they were
soon on the most intimate terms with it. They called
it 'Arthur.' Eventually, unable to stand it any
longer, they fired the thing. . . . I don't know at
what and I'm not at all sure they know themselves. . . ."

"Anyway," they said, "we've got rid of 'Arthur!' "

THE BRITISH ARMY IN TRAINING

This was written at the time of a visit to England in January, 1940.

I

INFANTRY

ONE of England's great strengths is that when she changes her methods, she does so within the old framework. Thus it is that she is a democracy within a monarchy; that her physicists win the Nobel prize from mediaeval universities; that having adopted conscription, for her a revolutionary decision, she enlists and trains her young soldiers in the old regiments which made up the former British Army. The Guards, the Warwicks, the Gordons, the Camerons and fifty others will each have, if need be, ten or fifteen battalions, and the youngsters of the new army inherit the traditions of the old.

There is, for instance, a training camp organized under the aegis of one of England's oldest and most famous regiments, the Queen's. Two thousand recruits are learning their jobs there. Amidst what two months ago was an ordinary, undistinguished countryside, comfortable, well-heated barracks have sprung up. All over the frozen fields the platoons are at work. Their instructors are those vertebrae of the Empire, the sergeants and sergeant-majors of The British Army—huge fellows, deep-chested, formidable of voice. One left his group at the double as soon as the Colonel appeared, and with a salute of frightening energy and a click of the heels, pulled up short and reported thunderously:

"Sergeant Hill, sir . . . Third platoon . . . Fifth week of training . . . Bayonet-charging, sir!"

As he listened, the Colonel looked the sergeant in the eyes. Each knew in what esteem the other held him. It was military grandeur, without servitude.

[218]

TRAGEDY IN FRANCE

We watched the training. It involved setting out in parties of four, rifle in hand, leaping a wall, fixing bayonets, running through a first bunch of hanging dummies, pinning to the ground a second representing riflemen lying on their stomachs, and finally taking a trench. It was all carried out in one frenzied movement. Sergeant Hill was like a man possessed. He set off with each new party, leaped the wall, shouted encouragement to his men, urged them onward and infused them with his own indefatigable enthusiasm.

They looked intelligent, these young soldiers, almost without exception. Every class of society was represented. The English peer was in the same platoon with the man who farmed his estate, the Oxford classical scholar in the same platoon with his butcher.

"Are you satisfied with them?" I asked the Colonel.

"More than that. I've never had better recruits. They are far better educated than the old-time soldier. And above all they are as keen as mustard . . . Just watch that platoon over there taking down and putting up a Bren gun. Many of them are discovering here for the first time the beauties of machinery, and they are fascinated by the discovery."

A second sergeant ran up. His heels clicked together; he saluted briskly.

"Sergeant Plews, sir," he thundered, "Fifteenth platoon, sir . . . Sixth week of training . . . Bren gun firing at moving target, sir!"

With the thermometer registering ten degrees below zero, the Colonel stood motionless, without a coat, warmed no doubt by the manifest zeal of those around him.

II

AVIATION

The Air Commodore in charge of a school for pilots was a very different person from the colonels of the land army. A born teacher, his touch was lighter, his discipline paternal. They were fine-looking boys, these pupils of his . . . *non Angli, sed Angeli.*

His school turned out hundreds of pilots a year.

"In nine months," he said, touching wood, "I've had only one accident."

[220]

In a vast hall stood two fuselages completely closed in and mounted on a complex system of transoms. The pupil is shut in and has before him all the normal controls and instruments of an airplane, with the earphones over his head. The instructor, who sits at a table not far from the machine, can communicate movements to the fuselage and move the needles of the instruments. He gives his pilot, by telephone, navigation instructions and informs him of anything incidental, like hills, airpockets, sights of enemy aircraft. The pupil must react properly. Everything he does is recorded. When he gets down from the fuselage, he is shown what he has done and reminded of what he should have done. This static navigation is safe and instructive.

Then there is the bombing course . . . On the floor of a darkened room is projected the film of some countryside as it would appear from an airplane flying at ten thousand feet. The pupil sits in a cage suspended from the roof and is provided with maps and bombing apparatus. The film moves over the ground at a speed corresponding to that of a landscape visible from an airplane flying at three hundred miles an hour. The pupil is given on the map before "taking off" an indication of the points to be bombed. During flight the release must be operated at the moment he thinks fit. A luminous signal on the plan shows where the bombs have fallen and immediately reveals the extent of error.

The talking picture is another auxiliary to instruction. The pupils are assembled in a projecting room. The film is a record of a reconnaissance flight. It starts with the moment the pilot is summoned by his superior officer and receives from him the plan and all necessary information.

"You will follow such and such a road, such and such a river . . . This is what we know of the enemy's positions . . . This is what we'd like to know."

"And now," the Commodore said, "Lord H——, who is one of our instructors, will show you the *camera obscura*."

This was a photographic chamber, about two yards square and situated in the middle of a field. In the center of the roof was a thick glass lens; under the lens on a table, a sheet of white paper. A pupil receives instructions to bomb a certain point. He goes up and as soon as he enters the field of the camera a tiny black airplane begins to move across the paper. The instructor follows it with a pencil and describes the trajectory it makes. Each time the pupil releases a bomb, he lights up beneath his machine one of those little magnesium lamps used by photographers. A point of light then appears on the white paper. When the pilot comes down again, the instructor is able to show him, with complete precision, the differences between the path he has followed and the path assigned to him, as well as the points where each bomb has fallen. It is a simple yet perfect method.

III

THE LARK

"These young pilots the Dominions are sending us," said the School Commander, "are splendid— and sometimes a little frightening. . . . The other day I sent one of them up to do his height test. . . . We forbade him to go over ten thousand feet without oxygen. . . . It was a marvellous day . . . sun shining, sky as blue as any sky of Italy. . . . Having got up there, my young Canadian was in-

[223]

toxicated with the purity of it all, like a lark or a poet, and he went on climbing. . . . Twelve thousand feet. . . . Fifteen thousand. . . . And then, I suppose, he lost his head and suddenly dived flat out. . . . They are told to straighten up when they get down to a certain height, but when descent is so rapid, the needle lags behind the machine, so my Canadian got almost to the ground at full speed. . . . When I saw the meteor approaching, my knees sagged a little and I said to myself: 'Poor little devil. . . . That's that. . . .' But that was not that. He landed with a shocking din of quivering stays and metal, without mishap. . . . Once reassured, I quite naturally lost my temper, had him brought in and said: 'All that was just silly. What good did it do? Now you've got an appalling headache.' 'Excuse me, sir,' he said, 'but I haven't a headache.' 'Well then, you've split an ear-drum?' 'I'm sorry, sir, but I haven't split an ear-drum.' 'Well, in any case, you've behaved in a most ridiculous manner!' 'I see that now, sir,' he said, 'but it was so lovely up there!'"

At that moment a young man saluted as he passed. "That is a rather curious case too," said the Commodore. "He is a young actor who, without ever having been in an airplane, played the part of a pilot in a propaganda film called 'The Lion Has Wings.' He liked the part so much that as soon as the film was finished he took up flying."

Which all goes to make excellent pilots.

IV

TANKS

The hangar was enormous, big enough to house attacking tanks, both heavy and light, and models of motors bisected to show how the machinery functioned. Everywhere groups of from eight to ten young men, separated by screens of stretched packing cloth, sat around tables on which lay detached machine pieces. Each man wore the mechanic's blue overall and the beret of our French *chasseurs alpine*. Each group had in its midst its instructor, a commissioned or non-commissioned officer.

"Blackwell, how many sparks to one complete revolution of the motor?"

What strikes the French visitor is first of all the quality of the instructors, the clarity of their explanations, the precision of their questions, their patience, even their indulgence. Then, the practical nature of the teaching. Of theory there is little or nothing. On the blackboards I saw a few sketches of machinery but never a mathematical formula, and both the instructor and his pupils were immediately more comfortable when they abandoned the blackboard for the object itself. These Anglo-Saxons have recognized the necessity of gaining a solid foothold on reality.

As soon as they know how to take down and assemble their arms, the men start their firing apprenticeship. Around a huge room ran a diorama representing a French countryside, with villages, steeples, isolated farms, haystacks, crossroads. In the midst of it all stood a tank with gun, gunner and, erect in the turret, a gun captain. A non-commissioned instructor indicated a point on the diorama to the gun captain.

"Here is a machine-gun opening fire on you. . . . You want to silence it. Give your orders."

The fair young head nodded vigorously.

"Left. . . . Ten o'clock." (The time indicated the position of the gun on an imaginary dial.) "A

black hedge two finger-breadths from the steeple.
. . . Range: 600 yards. Fire!"

The gun was innocent of a shell, but a pencil of
light struck the diorama at the point aimed at by
the gun at the moment of firing. . . . It was too
short.

"Another hundred yards. . . ."

The pencil of light fell on the hedge. The instructor chose another object.

"Right. . . . Half-past four. Range: 1200
yards. . . . West edge of the beetroot field. . . .
Fire!"

Such is the first course.

V

SHADOW-CHASING

We went into an adjoining room and found it
contained some curious-looking machines. They
were tanks stripped of their armouring and
mounted on oscillating transoms to give them the
see-saw motion that would be produced by rough
country. Before each of the tanks lay a stretch of
countryside, not painted this time on a circular can-
vas, but modelled in miniature on a long, earth-

covered platform. There were the little cardboard houses, the nursery railway lines and minute tanks moving over the ground. The *décor* reminded one of the models one sees in museums, while the armouring of the tanks, brought to life by bizarre and brutal movement, might have been something in Luna Park or Coney Island.

But this giant toy which would delight the heart of any small boy is only the instrument of an excellent method of instruction. Seated in his tank, with the butt of his gun at his right shoulder, his left eye on the sight, and shaken by the artificially-produced vicissitudes, the gunner works under what are almost the normal conditions of actual warfare. True, his gun does not fire real shells but it fires an air-gun which enables him to judge of the accuracy of his shooting. Tiny pellets strike the houses, the trains and the tanks. When, a little later, the young soldier is shaken by real ground and his gun fires real shells, surprise will be reduced to a minimum and familiarity a matter of moments. In just the same way the newcomer practices firing with a pencil of light at fast-flying aircraft that are only shadows moving across a white wall.

VI

FROM THE TABLE TO THE GROUND

Then the tactical course. The youngsters sat in a gallery that ran round a sand-covered table, whereon the instructor had modelled a contour to fit the tactical problem to be presented. In this countryside were three tiny tanks, to scale. From under the table three of the pupils acted as commanders and were provided with magnets which enabled them to steer the tanks across the sand.

"We have here," the instructor said, "a group of tanks on reconnaissance. . . . They have been told in the morning that their name for the day would be Argo. The group commander's tank is Argo A, the others Argo 1 and Argo 2. Argo A is a little way in the rear. The three tanks advance across the country. Advance. . . ."

Mysterious forces operated under the table and the tanks bounded onwards through the thickets.

"From the spinney here" (the instructor indicated it with his cane) "an anti-tank gun opens fire on Argo 1. Argo 1 immediately conceals itself with smoke-bombs and sends a wireless message to

[229]

the group commander. . . . What is the message.
. . . You, Beeton?"

"Argo 1 to Argo A . . . (The message followed).

"Good," said the instructor. "What is the commander's reply? You, Smith . . ."

The commander gave his orders. The tanks
moved over the sand. Headquarters intervened
from its depths. The pupils were completely im-
mersed in the game. Their replies seemed precise
and intelligent enough.

"Now," said the instructor, "you'll see the same
operation outside."

And soon we were in the snow and wind on the
crest of some rising ground that made me think of
the battles of Napoleon. Around us the fields and
woods, the pools and cliffs and great folds length-
ened by the snow stretched into an unseen distance.
This was God's table. But for what tragic game?
Soon there loomed over the hill a tank, a green,
stumbling monster. Then another, Argo 1 and
Argo 2 . . . And then, in the rear, according to
plan, Argo A . . . There was something satisfy-
ing to the mind in this change of scale. Suddenly,

surely enough, gunfire came from a spinney. Argo
1 threw down a smoke-bomb. Behind us a loud-
speaker began to splutter, tuned in with the radios
of the three tanks.

"Argo 1 to Argo A . . ."

Stage by stage the real maneuver followed the
phases of the imaginary one.

VII

FROM INDOOR TO OUTDOOR GUNNERY

The scene changed. Real firing called for a clear
field and the one chosen by headquarters was
ideally situated. It was a long valley flanked by a
cliff. Beyond it lay the sea. First of all we saw them
firing the smoke-mortar, which is amazingly effective. Three bombs saw the enemy completely blind-
folded.

Then a classic target, black and white, began to
run across the cliff. A tank manned by cadets
moved along the ridge on the opposite side of the
valley. The pupils fired machine-guns first and
then cannon. The shell was luminous and the red
ball made prodigious ricochets over the cliff. The
shooting was not perfect but very good considering

that it was the first of these exercises for the youngsters. Hitherto their only training had been with miniature targets and there was the kick of the cannon, the noise of the tank and the continuous buffeting to upset them. But the progressive method had given them confidence and they came through the test well enough. The target was quite often hit.

The shells bounded forward and reached on the edge of the slope the grass that the sea wind had dried. It caught fire and a ribbon of flame spread up to the snow. The pure fine lines of the cliff stood out against a bay of pale green closed by a long rock. The tanks ran on, their cannons sounding ceaselessly, the red bombs leaping on their way, while in the distance the cloud created by the mortar gradually unravelled itself.

Such was one of the schools of the Royal Tank Corps.

FIRST DAYS IN BELGIUM

This was written at the time of the attack in Belgium and of the subsequent retreat.

I

IT WAS strange, disturbing almost, to find the towns and villages that had teemed with British and French troops now practically deserted. In the line itself, work on the anti-tank ditches and blockhouses had ceased. Was it ever occupied, all this concrete? I wondered a little anxiously, and foolishly no doubt, imagined parachutists taking them over and harassing our own troops as they retreated. It looked to me then as if our armies had left for Belgium with such speed and confidence that nobody had any further thoughts for the back area.

And then I saw it on the march, this British Army that had been straining at the leash for so long in our villages of the North-East. Mighty indeed must have been its leap forward, with its hundreds of thousands of men, thousands of vehicles, guns and tanks, three hours after the order had been received. The roads I followed were just endless convoys. I saw not a single breakdown or stoppage. The traffic police, calm as if they had been in Piccadilly, were spaced along the pavements directing the moving columns quietly. Long, equal intervals separated the vehicles, making air attack difficult and ineffectual. As soon as a column halted for any reason, the men leaped down and positioned their anti-aircraft guns in the adjoining fields. Nearer the battle-line, I followed Scottish soldiers on foot, marching under the trees on either side of the road in widely separated platoons, like the attacking columns in the last war. They whistled a march as they swung along.

The welcome the Belgians gave to the French and British troops was magnificent. The inhabitants stood on the door-steps of every tiny village, every giant-belfried town. Young girls gave the soldiers flowers. "God be with you always!" they said. Lorries, armoured cars and tanks were covered with lilac. There and then the Belgian children learned the Tommies' gesture that ours had learned eight months before: "Thumbs up!" *"Tout va bien!"*

Those of the Belgian villagers who knew a few words of English used them to their best advantage. They said to the British officers through the windows of the cars: "I love you!" Even, magnificently, as the schoolmaster had said to Duncan (my British companion) that morning: Gentlemen you are the right men in the right place!" But almost all of them spoke to me in French. "You've not been very long coming," they said, amazed.

In accordance with orders, we followed the Tournai-Renaix-Audenarde road. Just before Brussels, a Belgian policeman diverted the lorries and tanks to the right and refused them permission to enter the city. Duncan, who had made up his mind to have lunch in Brussels, told our chauffeur to carry on and the policeman raised no objections. A few minutes later, we were outside the Hotel

Métropole. Here, to our great surprise, we were given an ovation. The crowd shouted "Vive la France! Vive l'Angleterre!" Women thrust flowers upon us and our car was soon a mass of them. Our chauffeur, a young Cockney, incapable of surprise, found himself beset by admirers and repeatedly kissed.

"What does all this mean?" I said to Duncan. "Why this triumphal reception? If we were generals or heroes or both I could understand it; but two unknown captains. . . ."

After lunch I went to the French Embassy and Madame Bargeton explained our triumph. Brussels, being an open town, was completely forbidden to troops, so we, who had gone in by mistake, were in all probability the first French and British officers to be seen on the boulevard. Thus our sensational and brief success.

"If it is allowed," Madame Bargeton said, "come again as often as you can and don't hesitate to bring your French and English friends with you. I shall be keeping open house for the duration of the campaign."

The campaign, as far as the French Embassy in Brussels was concerned, was to last three days.

II

Anybody who was in Belgium at this time must have been struck by the sudden and complete change in the attitude of the civilian population between the first and second days of the Battle. That first day we felt that Belgium was bringing to the struggle courageous and cheerful comradeship; on the second day we saw her gloomy and restless.

Soon we began to meet the refugees, exhausted and pitiful—women without shoes, thrown by the bombs into the streets just as they were, walking in silk or cotton stockings—bare-footed even.

"But you're not thinking of walking a hundred miles like that?" I said to some of them.

"Anything rather than be taken by the Germans."

There were some heartrending scenes. One woman, having noticed that our lorries and tanks were camouflaged with branches, had picked up four leaves and spread them neatly in line along the top of her baby-carriage. Village firemen had brought their families away on the fire-engines. Some old men were huddled together in a hearse, the feeblest of them stretched out in the place where the coffin goes.

[237]

We were suddenly held up at a road junction by a collection of large farm carts, horse-drawn and laden with dishevelled fugitives. It looked like one of the naïve school-book illustrations of the flight of the Gallo-Roman farmers before the invader. Above a dozen German aircraft were circling over the road. We stopped near a stream shaded by willows. Between the roadway and the stream in a semi-circle of hewn trees stood a Calvary. When they heard the sullen roar of the bombs bursting near at hand, the women scrambled down from the carts and came and knelt before the Cross. And soon a chorus of litanies mingled with the evil hum of the planes and the crash of explosions. The contrast between the softness of the countryside, the quiet charm of the rustic stream, the beauty of the prayers and the violent machine-made menace from the sky raised me above any thoughts of the danger. Suddenly an old woman in black came and clung to me, babbling in Flemish. All I could understand was:

"Alles verloren . . . alles verloren. . . ."

Alas, like her, we too were soon to say, "All is lost!"

[238]

Duncan, ever a cavalryman, went up to the peasant who had stayed at the head of the horses.

"They're very fine animals you have there," he said, "and well kept too."

"Yes," the man replied proudly, "with these horses I can find work anywhere."

"Can you feed them?"

"Don't you worry. They won't go short. I've brought more food for them than I have for myself."

The squadron dropped its last salvo and sped away. We were able to get on. The next village we went through had been hit. An old man was wiping the blood from a wound in his cheek, still smoking the cheroot stuck in his pipe.

"You've been wounded?"

"Looks like it, doesn't it?" he said, with a strong Belgian accent.

"Where did the bomb land?"

"At the bottom of my yard, right on the privies."

Then we passed the last columns of refugees. We were now in a zone completely emptied of inhabitants and it presented an extraordinary picture. The hamlets I had seen teeming with life on the day before were dead. A convent was burning on the plain to our right, the red flames leaping above its roof-tops. It was all unreal. The names of the villages painted on the signposts awoke memories of Waterloo. There were Mont St. Jean, Gennape, Hougoumont, La Haie Sainte. . . .

"Could that be the Ohain road over there?" I said to Duncan.

A moment later I read: *"OHAIN, 2 kilomètres."*

We had been told that the British troops would occupy a line along the Dyle, from Louvain to Wavre. After the evacuated area we did in fact meet a few British soldiers. They were busy digging trenches and laying telephone lines just as they had done in the back areas. There were not many of them and the plain looked deserted. Somewhere behind us a battery was firing. A sentry told us we could take our car no further. We continued on foot and came to a ridge that dominated a little valley. Here we found two Tommies sitting beside a machine-gun, eating bread and cheese. They got to their feet and saluted. Duncan spoke to them.

"What river is this?"

"The Dyle, sir."

"And what is that on the ridge opposite?"

"The Germans, sir."

Thus it was that Duncan and I, without knowing it, went into the thick of the Battle of Flanders.

ROYAL AIR FORCE

*This was written in June, 1940,
while staying with a squadron of the
Royal Air Force.*

IT WAS an illustrious squadron, with more than a hundred victories to its credit. The air-field was an air-field no longer. The machines were dispersed over a motley of plots out this way and that. These were the Hurricanes, those beautiful dragon-flies, incredibly swift, invincible. The mechanics were working under a sun so strong that most of them had stripped to the waist. On the outskirts of a wood, the pilots were awaiting orders. One of them, a slender, fair-haired boy of nineteen, with eyes of forget-me-not blue, recognised and stopped me.

"Surely you came to the training school in England about four months ago. . . ."

"You're quite right. And here you are in the thick of things?"

"Yes, I was lucky. I joined the squadron on the eighth of May, and two days after that the war started. . . ."

The Squadron Leader, who was with me, added:

"He's just brought down his third Heinkel. . . . He looks like making one of our best pilots."

The boy blushed. I asked him:

"Is it different from what you expected?"

"Yes, it is. Mainly because of the extraordinary speed at which everything goes on here. You are in the air with nothing around you but the sky. Suddenly a black speck appears, then ten, then thirty—and all at once you're in the middle of a great roaring swarm, swirling about you. You have a split second to choose a target and fire. Then they are gone and you're alone once again in an empty sky. . . . It might be a dream."

"It doesn't seem to leave you a great deal of time to distinguish your own machines from the enemy's."

"So little," the Squadron Leader said, "that we've had to enlarge and increase the markings painted on our machines. By the time this war began, we'd reduced them to practically nothing at all. It was a mistake. . . ."

He pointed out another pilot to me, he too fair and blue-eyed. He looked no more than sixteen.

"That one," he said, "was baptised the *Enfant Terrible* by a Frenchwoman in one of your villages and the nickname has stuck to him. There's no doubt he deserves it; he's certainly an *Enfant Terrible* to the Messerschmitts. . . . The lieutenant walking with him we call the Magister. It's he who keeps the Squadron's diary."

"Could I see it?"

"Yes, certainly."

They brought along a sort of large exercise book, and in it each evening, a few lines had been written in a peaceful, regular hand. I turned at once to the day they called "The First Day of War." There I read: "10th May. Lovely day, but we were awakened by a terrific din. Every gun around us was firing at once. We ran to the airdrome and took off immediately. Before breakfast was ready we had at least six bombers on the list. . . ."

The narrative continued, unconsciously heroic,

often ironical. "Another nice day. . . ." The Magister had got four himself, the *Enfant Terrible* five, the C.O. six or seven. A sergeant-pilot had come down in flames in the enemy lines, escaped, thanks to his parachute, got back as far as the Meuse, swam across it and rejoined his squadron. The following day he wrote to his mother: "I couldn't finish my letter yesterday—had too much work to do. But you needn't worry, for I had time to take some exercise and do a little swimming."

One day the patrol met a German squadron in far greater numbers. "The Messerschmitts," the diary said, "had the audacity to attack us, with disastrous results for them. . . ." Despite the flippancy of the diary's tone, the reader could tell how terrible that fortnight had been—men awakened at three in the morning, flying until nightfall, never landing except for petrol and ammunition.

"You must have been exhausted."

"We were so tired, it was all we could do not to fall asleep in our machines. . . . Fortunately our Vice Air Marshal came to inspect us. When he saw three days' growth of beard on most of us he understood without our saying a word and had pilots sent out from England to relieve those who couldn't carry on."

"And the others?"

"We've had a little rest and it'll do. . . . Excitement keeps you going and this is the most exciting sort of big-game hunting."

"And what are your losses?"

"They don't really amount to much. We've lost machines, which have been replaced immediately, but very few pilots. The bombers have suffered more than we have. As for the Germans. . . ."

On the outskirts of the wood, in the shade of the young trees, a mechanic, stripped to the waist, had spread out the Squadron's flag. For every German plane brought down he was painting a tiny, black swastika.

THE SPIRIT OF FRANCE

A BROADCAST FROM LONDON, JUNE 18TH, 1940

I HAVE been asked to talk to you of the Spirit of France and, at first, yesterday, I hesitated to accept. The terrible events of the last few days made it painful for me to think of the glory that was, and that will be, France. I felt very much as a man who loves his wife dearly, and who sees her mortally ill. He would rather avoid talking about her, not because he loves her less, but on the contrary, because he realises better than ever how desperately he loves her and how great is the danger of losing her. However, if some friend gently, tenderly, succeeds in breaking his silence, very soon he understands that, though it hurts, it does him good all the same to talk about his beloved. Therefore I shall attempt to talk to you of my beloved France as if she was not to-day in so sad a condition, in so desperate a plight.

I shall always remember what I felt when I came back from America, for the first time, and went by train through Normandy, from Havre to Paris. I hadn't seen France for many months; it was as if I suddenly rediscovered her. "How lovely!" I thought. "This is not a country, it is a garden." And it is quite true that France is such an old country, and has been cultivated by her people for such a long time, with such loving care, that it really looks like one huge garden. When her continental neighbours, as it has unfortunately so often happened in history, thought and said: "The distribution of wealth is unfair; the French have got all the good and fertile land; we've got the marshes and the forests," they forgot that, for two thousand years, and more, Frenchmen had been clearing the forests and draining the marshes. And even now, how hard they work! Kipling used to say that France is a country where every man, woman, child and dog works from morning to night, and seems to enjoy it. That is certainly true of French peasants, and most French families come from peasant stock. It is from their farmer fathers that hard-working French professors and students learnt their devotion to their task.

And their farmer fathers respect them for being learned young men. No country in the world has more reverence than France for a good literary education. Every middleclass Frenchman knows at least some of his classics by heart; he has been brought up on La Fontaine, and Corneille, and Molière. The Comédie-Française, which is the national theatre, and the French Academy, are public institutions, and a surprisingly great part of the nation takes an interest in their ceremonies. Very often in the course of the last fifty years, France was governed by professors. Whether it was a sound idea or not is another story, but it is a fact, and it shows the great importance attached by Frenchmen to classical eloquence, to the proper use of words, to simple and beautiful language.

The French language has become, after centuries of improvement, so crystal clear that Lord Salisbury used to say that things would go better in the

world if it was forbidden to write about meta-
physics in any language other than French. It is
also the ideal language to talk about sentiments. In
the seventeenth and eighteenth centuries, at the
courts of the last Kings of France, idle men and
women of infinite subtlety took pleasure in analys-
ing very minutely each other's feelings and
thoughts. The result was this wonderful literature
that goes from La Bruyère and Pascal to Stendhal
and Marcel Proust. France became a country of
very refined taste. The part played by her in mod-
ern Europe was in a way similar to that played by
Greece in the ancient world; she took pleasure in a
delicious simplicity. Other literatures may have
had more strength, more romantic violence; none
had that mysterious perfection.

This was true, not only of literature, but of all the
arts. During the last dreadful days, as is only too
natural, as soon as I had a free moment, I let my
thoughts wander to France. What were then the
images that crossed my mind? It was the Place
Vendôme, the Place des Vosges, the Place de la
Concorde, all so well planned, so pure in design,
so simple in ornament. The whole world has praised

the good taste of the Paris working girls who, in the celebrated street that crosses the Place Vendôme, design dresses and jewels. Their taste comes, for a very large part, from the town in which they have been brought up. How could they have bad taste when, ever since they were children, they saw the lovely and simple lines of so many noble monuments? Even the light of Paris is just what it should be. There is never too much of it. A blue mist rises from the river and softens the corners of the grey stones of the Louvre, and outside Paris, what is more delightful than a French river with its poplar trees, or than one of those long and straight French roads above which the well-clipped trees build an endless green cathedral?

The people themselves, men and women, are sometimes, in France, works of art. God knows we have our bores and knaves like every nation. But many Frenchmen, in the happy days of peace, had turned life into a fine art. What could be more delightful than to dine with a few well-chosen friends, in a small Paris restaurant? The owner, who was called the *Patron*, was, of course, at the same time, the *chef*. He wasn't so much interested in your money as in your appreciation of his great talents. He wasn't a tradesman, but an artist and a friend. And the guests were often worthy of the setting. Paris conversation at its best was witty, brilliant, sometimes deep, never ponderous, sparkling with anecdotes, portraits and sketches of the great.

I remember suddenly a dinner which was offered to me, a few days before the German offensive, at the front, by some young French officers who formed the staff of a reconnaissance squadron. They all knew that they hadn't much of a chance to survive. They never said a word about it; they spoke gaily and brilliantly. Every one of them has now been killed. But we have a right to say that they were worthy of their fathers, the soldiers of the Marne. What has defeated them is a vastly superior material strength. We owe it to them to say that the spirit of France was never more alive than it was in them. It will live in their sons. No one can kill in a few months, or even years of occupation, a spirit that has been built by generation after generation of patient and faithful men and women.

TRAGEDY IN FRANCE

From the friends of France who listen to-day, I would ask two things. The first is: Do not judge France harshly in this hour of her great distress. She needs more than ever your understanding friendship and she has, I think, a right to it because she has lost everything in the service of freedom. The second is this: Take to-night the French book you prefer and read a few pages of it. Open a portfolio and ask Manet and Cézanne, Renoir and Degas, to refresh your memories of France. Then think of the French man or woman you like best, of an old mill in Provence, of an apple orchard in Normandy, of the bookshops on the quais of Paris, of some beautiful, long, rolling sentence in Chateaubriand's memoirs, of a blue sky, of a soft French voice, and the Spirit of France will be alive in you, as it is, this very minute, in the minds of millions of Frenchmen, who suffer for France and worship her.

Set in Linotype Caslon
Format by A. W. Rushmore
Manufactured by the Haddon Craftsmen
Published by HARPER & BROTHERS
New York and London